MY LIFE OF HELL AND HAPPINESS

My Life of Hell and Happiness

Emily Rogers

JANUS PUBLISHING COMPANY LTD
Cambridge, England

First published in Great Britain 2013
by Janus Publishing Company Ltd
The Studio
High Green
Gt Shelford
Cambridge CB22 5EG

www.januspublishing.co.uk

British Library Cataloguing-in-Publication Data
A catalogue record for this book is available from the British Library

ISBN 978-1-85756-802-8

Cover Design: Jackie Staines

Printed and bound in the UK by PublishPoint
from KnowledgePoint Limited, Reading

The story of my life as I know it and from what I have been told.

23 March 2012

To my adopted mum, Margaret C. Richardson,
and my late son, Jeremy Turner.

Contents

Acknowledgements	xi
Early Memories	1
The Mother I Loved	6
An Eerie Experience	13
The Mother Who Gave Birth to Me	16
The Start of It All	19
In Denial	23
My Sister	27
Scottish Horizons	30
My First Proper Relationship	34
The Early Years	40
Light at the End of the Tunnel	49
Seven Year Itch/Married Bliss?	52
Signpost of Sorrow	57
Old Haunts	65
Life Goes On, or Does It?	69
New Beginnings	79
Mary's Troubles	84
Missing and On the Run	87
Challenging Times Ahead	99
A Wish Comes True	103

Uncle Henry and Auntie Pat	105
Nana and Grandad Chaplin	107
Moving On	116
Angie, My Adopted Daughter	120
Grandchildren	122
Dreams Fulfilled and Camel Mania	126
Foreign Horizons	129
David's Cats	133
My New Families in Egypt	136
Living My Dream	141
You Can Choose Your Friends, But Not Your Family	147

Acknowledgements

I would like thank the following people for all their help and encouragement during the writing of this book. First, my publisher, Janus Publishing Company. Claire Pickering, without whose help this book would not have got off the ground. Peter, who told me I could write a book when he gave me a reading at church. Ray, Irene, Gloria, June, Jenny, Sean, my adopted family and lastly, Bernard, who sadly passed away on my birthday on 24 February 2012. They were always there in my time of need. Most importantly, I would like to thank my husband, David, who sometimes got neglected when I was writing this book. Without him I would be lost.

Any proceeds from the sale of this book will be donated to the poor villages and children, Egypt.

Early Memories

I emerged into this world on 24 February 1939 at Selly Oak Hospital, Birmingham. My mother is Mrs Blanche Edith Cynthia Granger, née Chaplin. I was three months premature, weighing just 3 lb 6 oz, and I was immediately placed in an incubator. Not expected to survive, I was baptised Emily after the nurse who delivered me. My middle names were added later – Joanne after my aunt and I am unsure where Jean came from. I was told it was a very cold and snowy day and that my mother was unaware of my birth as she was very ill with pneumonia.

Once we had been discharged from hospital we returned to my grandparents' home, Tom and Maria Grainger. (You may have noticed that I have spelt the surname differently, but I will explain the reasoning behind this later as my story unfolds.) They lived at 30 Foxwell Road, Bordesley Green, East Birmingham. Later that year my mother and I left England to join my father, David Granger, in India where he was serving in the British Army.

We lived in India until I was about 15 months old. Apparently we visited the Taj Mahal and several other places of interest which I was too young to remember. When we returned to England our ship was torpedoed, but fortunately all the babies were brought up from the sleeping area and the cradles were floatable.

My next home was in Luton, where my baby brother was born on 14 February 1941 – Valentine's Day. He was named David John Granger, but we called him by his second name because it got confusing as my father was of the same name and when called, they would both answer. Later, we called him Johnny.

I understand we then lived in Key Road in Clacton-on-Sea in Essex. We didn't stay there long as my mother came home one day and saw three mice sitting near the fire. Apparently she ran hell for leather and never went back.

We then moved into 59a Dudley Road in the next street near to my other grandparents, who lived at number 87 just down the road, also in Clacton-on-Sea. My grandmother was called Edith Millicent Chaplin and my grandfather was Rodney Gladstone Chaplin.

One of my earliest memories was being sent to live at 30 Foxwell Road with my brother in 1943, where we lived with my grandmother, Little Nan (we called her this as she was a little shorter than our other nan), and Aunt Daisy until the war was over because my mother didn't want us around. According to my uncle, who was more of a brother to us, being only five years older than I was, she was more interested in the American soldiers over at the stables at the back of where she still lived in Dudley Road. I distinctly remember the big old armchair with the black grate in the fireplace, the oven, the old green dresser in the corner and the dining table and chairs in the bay window. There was also a settee and a sideboard at the back.

My grandfather had passed away by this time so my brother and I never knew him. He was never spoken about and there were no photographs around. To this day we know nothing about him; apart from that he was a drunk who raised budgies and raffled the same one week after week around the different pubs. He was also a heavy gambler. It is believed he may have been of mixed race as all the boys in the family, including my own, had very dark skin which turned darker in the sun.

This was one of the happiest times of my life, with the exception of when my father came home on leave. It was in Birmingham at my nan's house that the first sexual contact started at 3 years old. Whenever he came home on leave he stayed at Nan's house; he never went home to my mother's while I was living with my nan – I guess the lure was too strong.

My brother and I both loved our nan, although she could be very strict and she meant what she said. I remember one occasion when we were sent over to the playing fields not far from where we lived. We were given a big bottle of water and told not to come back until dinner time.

I remember having a great time playing with the other kids, until I was playing on the big slide one day, when one of the boys pushed me before I was ready. On the way down I caught my knicker leg on something and they ripped across the crotch, exposing my Mary Jane to all and sundry. When I got home not only did I get a backhander for coming home early, but I also got another two: one for ripping my knickers and one for leaving my little brother at the playing fields. I was about 5 years old at the time and my brother was three.

On Saturday mornings we used to go to the ABC picture house to see showings like *Mickey Mouse, Old Mother Riley, Roy Rogers, Hopalong Cassidy* and other such films. I liked the cowboy films best and still do. But best of all, I liked the organ that came up from the floor so we could have a sing-song. My favourite song was 'We are the Ovaltineys, Little Girls and Boys'.

If we were good, on Saturday afternoon Nan would send me to the shop just across the tram lines. I had to be very careful as there were no traffic lights then. I used to take a big jug to fetch home-made ice cream and I can still taste it when I think about it now!

My best friend was Janet Beasley, who lived next door. Nan used to make us soap bubbles in a bowl and give us little clay pipes and home-made toffee apples. We used to sit on the step outside the privy for hours or play ball on the wall in the front garden or do handstands. We sometimes played with a girl called Margery Bennett who lived across the road and when it was cherry season we would climb the tree to scrump for cherries.

I remember VE Day very clearly. There were street parties in every road from one end to the other. All the families pulled together in those days and you could leave your doors unlocked – not like today. I also remember my brother getting a smack across the ear for calling out 'Daddy' to a soldier coming up the road – poor kid nearly fell off his chair. It was actually my uncle Reuben and they looked very alike, so he could be forgiven for making this mistake.

I am not sure when rationing came to an end, but I do remember that one day, when I was ill in bed, the doctor came to see me and he told my parents that I had to go on a diet as I was overweight; I still am. In those days we were only allowed 4 oz of sweets a week. It was a Saturday morning and my friend Olive Palmer came round to our house to see how I was. She had just spent the last 2 oz of her sweet coupons and bought me some humbugs. When I told her I had been put on a diet, she stuffed them under my pillow and told me to eat them when I was on my own – bless her! I gave her my word that when I grew up I would buy her something special. I kept my promise and when I went to visit her in America years later I took a gold dolphin necklace and earring set. We laughed about it at the time as she had forgotten all about it until I reminded her.

When the ration books had to be renewed it was always Olive and me who had to go and queue up at the town hall. We were gone for ages as we had to get Nan's as well. On Saturday mornings Olive and I would go shopping for Nan to get the meat and veg. We also had to go to the bakers for bread and a dozen crispy rolls. When we got back Nan would put cheese in the rolls and put them in the old black fire range to heat them up so we could have hot cheese rolls and a hot drink. She also used to give us a penny or tuppence to spend. You could get quite a lot with it in those days.

My first school was Alston Primary in Bordesley Green. We were still living with Nan Grainger at the time as it was during the war years. One of my first memories of school is being in the hall, dancing to music, when a boy kissed me with a twisted mouth. Another time I was on my way home from school one day when I got tar on my new green dress made of organza, which is like a sort of chiffon, as the road had just been resurfaced. Not wanting to receive the inevitable backhander, which would surely be waiting for me when she found out, I didn't exactly hurry home that day.

In 1946, at around 7 years old, I was sent to Joyce Snowdon's School of Dancing for ballet, tap and acrobat lessons, which I liked. I was quite good at all three lessons and passed all the exams that I took. I had lots of certificates; although I don't know what has happened to them now as my mother kept hold of them.

I made friends with a girl called Naomi who lived in the same street. Her mother was good at dressmaking and made all our costumes. We even joined in at a carnival on a float one year. Another year that sticks in my mind was when we had a production at the Princess Theatre, which was inside Clacton Town Hall; it is still there today. We were all on stage in our lovely costumes doing the Skater's Waltz, when all of a sudden my knicker elastic broke and down fell my knickers. All I could do was to kick them to the back of the stage and carry on dancing. My family were in the audience and Grandad heard a man in front of him make a comment to someone about it. He wasn't at all happy and apparently he told the man he was supposed to be watching the show and not looking at little girls' knickers.

I went to the Baptist church in Clacton and regularly attended Sunday school, where each year you could take an exam about the Bible. We used to have lessons each week with our Sunday school teacher, who worked in a butcher's shop called Dewhursts in Pier Avenue in Clacton. Lessons would be held either at the back of the shop or at his family home. I was good at this subject and if you passed three years running you had your name engraved in gold lettering in the entrance hall to the main church. I was always interested in the Scriptures and passed each exam with top marks. I was so pleased to see my name up there.

I also joined the Girls' Life Brigade (GLB) at the church, where I met a lady who was to play a big part in my life. We met at a party that we were holding and why she took to me I don't know, but I was ever so grateful as later on in life she became the mother I never really had.

The Mother I Loved

I loved the lady who adopted me in later life for the daughter she had always wanted and I came to know her as 'Mum'. We first met when I was 10 years old in 1949 at a Girls Life Brigade party at the Baptist church in Clacton-on-Sea and I have loved her ever since. Her name was Margaret Richardson and I used to call her Auntie Margaret. At the time I was living at the flat in Dudley Road with my parents, which was within walking distance to the church building where the GLB meetings were held on a Monday evening.

The following year in 1950 I moved to North Road with my parents, my brother, Johnny, and a new baby sister. This meant I had to travel to church and the GLB by bus. Auntie Margaret was twelve years older than I was, which would make 'Mum' 22 years old at the time. She lived in a village 2 miles away called Little Clacton with her own mother at a cattery and kennels called Sunny Corner Kennels. We used to meet on the bus as it was the same route to the GLB. I got to know her better over time and she used to take me for something to eat and drink afterwards as we had an hour to wait for the bus. She became a GLB officer and after the meetings on Monday nights she would take me to the milk bar and we would have real crab sandwiches and a drink before we caught the nine o'clock bus home. I would get off at Great Clacton and she would carry on to Little Clacton. Sometimes we went to Davey's Restaurant and I would have Welsh rarebit (cheese on toast). Those days were really special to me.

As Auntie Margaret got to know me better, she asked my parents if she could take me to the evening service on a Sunday. She used to give me a silver sixpence to put in the collection plate. She also took me out during the school holidays when she didn't have to work. I always looked forward to seeing her. During these outings I was in a different world and I wished she was my real mum and that I didn't have to go back to the real world to live with my parents. I remember the time when she took me and my brother out one summer evening onto Clacton Pier and gave us the time of our lives. We went on everything that we were able to and went home with lots of prizes that we had won and presents that were bought for us.

Leading up to 1953 and the coronation year of Queen Elizabeth, Auntie Margaret asked me if I would like to be baptised at the Baptist church, where the minister immersed you in water like John the Baptist had done to Jesus. I had already been christened at birth as I was premature and not expected to live. Auntie Margaret said it was not like being baptised properly, so I said I would think about it and that I would have to speak to my parents first. When I next met her I told her my parents had agreed and so she arranged for me to go to the meetings so I could learn what being baptised meant. There were other people who were also going to be baptised, but I was the youngest and so Auntie Margaret always came with me.

The group would meet at the minister's home and Auntie Margaret was responsible for getting me back safely to my parents. Auntie Margaret knew the minister, Dr Riddle, and his wife well and we were asked to stay behind to have a talk and to have coffee and sandwiches at the end of the meetings. I remember one evening I was late leaving the minister's home. The evening had gone quickly and it was after eleven o'clock before we realised the time. I couldn't phone my parents as they weren't on the phone, so Dr Riddle drove us there and Auntie Margaret said she would escort me to the door to tell my parents that it was her fault I was late.

On the way home we passed my father, who was out looking for me. We stopped the car to wait for him to catch up so that Dr Riddle could take us all the rest of the way home. I thought my father was going to be cross, but he seemed fine with it; he had just wondered where I was at that time of night. Dr Riddle gave my father a card with his phone number on it, in case he wanted to get in touch if it was getting late in the future and I still wasn't home.

By the time we got in my mother had gone to bed and like every night, he forced sex on me again, standing between the back room and the hall, ruining an otherwise wonderful evening. Auntie Margaret was extremely angry when she found out about what my father had done to me when I was younger and I suppose now that I should have told her earlier and she would have tried to do something about it.

The baptism was in June 1953 and Auntie Margaret bought me a New Testament, which she signed on the front of the front cover; I still have it now, along with the one that she bought for me when she bought my son Jeremy's before he passed into the next world.

On my birthdays and at Christmas time Auntie Margaret would take me out for dinner and this continued into my adulthood. She still worries about me now and yet it is me who should be worrying about her now she has gone into a residential hotel, having had three heart attacks. The man who owns the home is well known in the upper classes and Auntie Margaret is a friend of his mother. I believe Auntie Margaret's mother mixed with the higher members of society, but really they were no different to me, apart from having lots of money and speaking properly. Even they still have to go to the toilet, the same as everybody else. Most of them were born with a silver spoon in their mouths, except for the few who worked hard to get where they were. Well good luck to them, I say. I don't begrudge those sorts of people, but some of them turn up their noses at those who aren't so fortunate as themselves, but just because they have money doesn't mean they are any better than anyone else.

When Auntie Margaret's mother passed away in the 1960s, Auntie Margaret was left quite a considerable amount of money in her will. Auntie Margaret is a very giving person and she never let anyone treat her to a meal or take her out for the day. She had plenty of friends, whom her mother had introduced her to over the years when the kennels were open, most of whom lived in a small seaside town called Frinton-on-Sea. Her own mother hadn't paid any national insurance contributions when she had worked for her, perhaps thinking Auntie Margaret would be able to live on the money that was left to her when she died. But because Auntie Margaret spent a lot of her inheritance treating other people, not thinking about the future or when she retired, she had to rely on the benefit system, which she felt ashamed about.

I knew it was a large amount Auntie Margaret had inherited because she had told me and I felt very uncomfortable when she asked me not to tell anyone that she was living on the benefit system once it had all gone. Auntie Margaret was only getting £29 a week to live on and she showed me her allowance book before the system changed to the plastic cards we now use. I wanted to help her as I was now in the position to do so, but she wouldn't let me. I wanted to be able to thank her for being the best 'mum' I could ever have had and for all the love she had given me, but she was too proud to accept help.

After a while the system changed and made the money up to what it should be when you reach retirement age. While Auntie Margaret had the bungalow to live in that her own mother had left her, she still had bills to pay. Auntie Margaret wasn't used to budgeting as her mother had always done this, so it came as quite a shock. At the time Auntie Margaret was still taking friends out to lunch, so no one knew how little money she really had to live on. I would always offer to pay my share of the bill whenever she took me out, but she wouldn't hear of it. The only way I could repay her was to send her money on her birthday and at Christmas. I would also buy her things that she needed like writing paper and envelopes, even putting postage stamps in the letters I wrote. These were little things, I know, but I knew that she would make good use of them and it was the only way I could see to help out. She often told me off for doing so, but it went in one ear and out of the other, as I still kept on doing it.

After Auntie Margaret had had her heart attacks and went into the nursing home I was able to send her many parcels with all the things that she needed. When she found out that she wouldn't be going back to the bungalow, she had to put it up for sale to pay back the money the benefit system had paid out for the nursing home fees. She had fallen behind with the fees when she'd had her benefits stopped, when they discovered she had property.

On Monday, 9 May 2011, the bungalow was finally sold. Auntie Margaret was sad as she had very happy memories there, having lived there most of her life. It had been up for sale for months and was bought by the owner of the nursing home, where Auntie Margaret was now living. All that had to be done now was for the papers to be signed and the keys handed over.

Auntie Margaret was a hoarder and she never threw anything away, so whoever bought the property would have their work cut out. At the time I was unable to do any clearing as I couldn't stand for long or carry anything with my increased disabilities. Just before Easter of 2011, Auntie Margaret had a nasty fall and broke her pelvis. She was taken to the general hospital in Colchester. When I was informed of the fall I immediately went to see her. She looked very ill and was in a lot of pain. She could hardly move and was so pleased to see me. She wanted to know why I had taken so long to visit her in hospital and I explained that I had only received the letter that day, from one of her friends who had written to me.

I visited Auntie Margaret day and night, unless she had other visitors, which she usually did in the afternoons. She wasn't eating or drinking and neither was she taking her medication. Every evening she would hand me a load of pills to get rid of, swearing me to secrecy, putting me in an awkward position. But she knew she could rely on me as we were very close to each other. She often confided in me and she told me that she wouldn't be going back to the nursing home when she came out of hospital.

On the evening of Friday, 13 May I went to see her in hospital. She'd had visitors all afternoon and was smiling and looking a lot better. She was happy and relieved to have been able to sort out her money worries before she passed away. The conversation turned to her funeral and I asked her what colour she wanted me to wear – her favourite colour blue, or black. I had bought a black outfit just recently when she told me she was going to die and that she wasn't coming out of hospital, as I didn't want to have to rush around at the last minute. It was just like having an everyday conversation with her, but I was determined it would be a long time yet before I had to wear it. She asked me what it was like and I told her I would start off with black underwear, black tights, a pair of black trousers, a black top with a black cardigan and black shoes. She asked me if I had a handbag and I said that I did. Then she asked if I was going to wear a hat as I normally didn't like wearing them. I said that on this occasion I would break tradition and borrow one as I knew someone who had one who would lend it to me. It was so nice to see her laughing and in good spirits as she hadn't laughed so much for a long time.

I left her at 9 o'clock after visiting time had finished and we kissed each other goodbye. I said I would see her next the day – Saturday. I had arranged to go to a fete in the morning with my adoptive daughter, Angela, who was going to pick me up at 9.30 a.m. We both wanted to be back by lunch as I was going to the hospital and Angela was having friends round. It was a lovely sunny day and a good time was had by all.

When we got back I had time to have a snack and get changed, before the taxi came to pick me up at 1.30 p.m. Half an hour beforehand, the phone rang. I picked it up and the voice at the other end asked if they could speak to Mrs Brassell.

'Speaking,' I replied.

'This is the general hospital. I am so sorry; your mum has just passed away. We tried to resuscitate her but were unable to save her.'

'Thank you,' I said.

'Do you want to come and see her?' the voice asked.

'No thank you,' I replied. 'I'll go and see her when she's at the chapel of rest. Thank you for letting me know. Goodbye.'

When I put the receiver down, I stood there in a trance-like state trying to take in what I had just been told. It was David who brought me out of the trance, asking who was on the phone. All I could do was burst into tears. David knew that even though she wasn't my birth mother, I loved her very much.

About ten minutes later the phone rang again. The voice at the other end asked if I was Mrs Brassell and I said that I was. I was then told that I would have to phone the bereavement suite on the Monday to make arrangements over what would happen next as there was to be an autopsy before the body could be released. I explained that her executor would be seeing to all the arrangements for the funeral. It was then that I was told I was down as her second next of kin and that I was to be informed. I thanked the person and then rang off. Unbeknown to me, Auntie Margaret had put my name down as the second next of kin in her will.

On the Monday I tried to get through to the bereavement suite at the hospital all day but couldn't, so I left it, hoping that her executor had been informed of her death. I phoned the hospital to ask if they could let me have the name and phone number of her executor and after I had explained who I was, the nurse was very helpful and rang through to the ward where she had been treated. I was informed that the executor's name was Mr Bell, so I rang him and he answered the phone. I explained that I was Emily, Peggy's adoptive daughter; 'Mum' was always known as Peggy by those who knew her best.

Mr Bell informed me that he was unable to let me know any details as the undertaker was away on holiday. He asked if I would ring back on Thursday evening on 28 May, when he would have been to see the undertaker, at which point he would be able to give me the time and date of her funeral. I thanked him and put the phone down.

I knew she was having a church service before the cremation as we had spoken about it prior to her death when she asked if I would be able to go. She very much wanted me to go but knew it would be a little awkward getting there as it meant I would have to catch a bus from Colchester to Clacton and then from Clacton to Thorpe-le-Soken, a small village. I told her not to worry and that I would be there, even if I had to hire a taxi for the day. But as it turned out I wouldn't need to as Angela, my adoptive daughter, agreed to take me.

The funeral was organised for 7 June 2011 at Thorpe Church at one o'clock and then afterwards at the crematorium. I asked Mr Bell if it would be all right if I went to see my 'mum' at the chapel of rest and agreed to phone the funeral parlour to find out. He rang me back to tell me it was at Clacton and gave me the number to ring, so I phoned the next morning on the Friday. I was informed that if I wanted to see her it would have to be no later than the following morning. After that it wouldn't be possible as the body would have started to deteriorate.

I made an appointment for ten o'clock then phoned Angela to ask if she would drop me off at the funeral parlour. She agreed but didn't want to come in with me as she wanted to remember her how she was the last time she had seen her when we had all gone out for lunch together. Instead, she said she would take her dog, Hope, for a walk along the seafront.

An Eerie Experience

When I arrived at the undertakers I explained who I was. The lady and gentleman were very nice. They knew 'mum' well and said all the staff were very sorry for my loss and that Mum would be missed by all who had known her. The gentleman showed me into the chapel of rest and I was told to take as long as I needed before being left to it.

Mum looked so peaceful lying there in the coffin. All the pain had gone from her face and she looked as if she was sleeping, dressed in her new blue nightdress with her hair neatly combed and a little make-up on her face. I kissed her gently then sat on a chair beside her. I said a prayer, knowing how she would be happy now that she was reunited with her own mum. Then I sat talking to her, going over the past years we had known each other – all the places we had been, the laughs and the tears, and all the happy and sad times we had both shared. The funeral director had put cards on a small table so the visitors could write a message to their loved ones and seal them in the envelope, so I wrote a letter to put in the coffin with her.

I sat with her for nearly an hour, then I stood up, bent over the coffin and kissed her for the last time. The next fifteen minutes were very weird. It wasn't frightening because I'm a spiritualist, but when I went to open the door, it wouldn't budge, no matter how hard I tried. I knew that I hadn't been locked in there as there was no lock on the door, so I knocked on the door loudly to get some attention, but no one came. I tried again but still nothing happened, so I sat down again and spoke to my mum, asking her to let me out of the little room where she was resting peacefully. I knew it must have something to do with the spirit world, as there couldn't have been any other explanation. I have had several experiences like this before, with things being moved or going missing. I then remembered the last evening when I was with her at the hospital and she had held my hand tightly, asking me to stay longer after visiting hours had finished. 'Mum' must have known that she was going to leave this earthly plane. You are supposed to know when it is your time to leave and I'd had experience of this before when Jeremy had asked me to buy some new clothes for his last birthday, telling me they were for something special; he had later died.

I tried the door again but it still wouldn't open, so I knocked once more then sat back down on the chair and waited. After a few minutes there was a knock on the door. It was the undertaker who had come to see if I was all right, as I had been quite a while. I told him I couldn't open the door and that I had knocked several times before he came. We walked back to the office, where the assistant was still at her desk busy writing. The undertaker explained what had happened and they both laughed, telling me they had both heard the knocking and thinking it was someone at the front door, they went to see if anyone was trying to get in. The main door had been locked because it was early closing on a Saturday, but there was no one there. After trying the back door, they both wondered if they had laid a body out and the person was still alive, thinking the knocking was coming from the room next door to the office.

Next door was a florist, so I went in to order flowers for 'Mum's' funeral. It made sense to order them there as it would save me having to look for a flower shop when I was back in Colchester, where many of the shops had closed down. I picked a wreath with the word Mum on it in white chrysanthemums with blue irises in the corner, trimmed with baby blue ribbon – Mum's favourite colour.

I made my way back to the car park behind the undertakers and Angela asked if I was all right. I told her about being locked in the room with 'Mum'. Angela is a spiritualist and a medium, and she told me that it was 'Mum' in the spirit world, wanting me to stay with her a little longer, which I had already known. Nana Chaplin always told me that God works in mysterious ways.

On the morning of the funeral I got up early to shower, wash my hair and get ready for Angela to pick me up. Angela had decided that she wasn't going to be coming in to the church, so I was feeling nervous because there would be people at the funeral I didn't know. A lot of the mourners were from well-to-do families, but I wasn't going to let them think I was a nobody. I wasn't going for the posh mourners, I was going for my mum. Yes! My mum. I was going to make 'Mum' proud of me. I was glad that 'Mum' wasn't like them.

Angela picked me up at 12 noon and we arrived early, so we stayed in the car until some more mourners arrived. As I began to walk towards the church, Angela called out to let me know that someone was asking after me. It was a friend of 'Mum's' called Venetia, who lived in Kent. I was so pleased to see a friendly face. She often visited 'Mum', even when she was at the nursing home. She used to live in the village of Little Clacton, not far from where 'Mum' was living. I had known Venetia nearly as long as I had known 'Mum', when I was still at school.

Her son had come with her and the three of us walked to the church entrance, where we waited for the hearse to arrive, as we were the chief mourners. It was a lovely service and the vicar spoke very highly of 'Mum'. We followed the hearse to the crematorium, taking the road past where 'Mum' had lived, where we paused for a few minutes outside the bungalow before moving on. All the mourners were already seated in the crematorium and as one of the chief mourners, I led the procession with 'Mum's' adopted daughter and the rest followed as we were escorted to the front pew for the last part of mum's funeral.

'Mum' had so many flowers that they were laid out on the lawn, as Weeley Crematorium only had a small space in which to lay flowers from each of the mourners. The wreath I had bought had been placed in the middle so that it stood out amongst the other wreaths and flowers. The funeral had gone well and I knew in my heart that 'Mum' would be proud of me.

The Mother Who Gave Birth to Me

Mother – well, what can I say about her? Nothing nice, anyway. Right after my birth, when she was able to see me, she hated me for ruining her life. Mother liked the good time, but not the consequence of her actions, resulting in me being born. She never loved my father – he was just a bit of fun as far as she was concerned. Mother was a bit naive about sex and in those days, young girls weren't told about things such as how a baby was conceived or how they were born. Right up until I was born, Mother thought that you were simply cut open to get the baby out. I don't know how Mother thought babies got there in the first place. I should have felt sorry for her in a way, as in the early 1920s that generation didn't really know about having babies until it actually happened; although I would have thought that any good mother would have passed their knowledge on to their daughters.

Mother was only a child herself really, when she fell pregnant with me at the age of 16. When I was old enough to know, relatives informed me how young she was at the time. Had she not treated me in the way that she did, I might have felt some sympathy for her. She was always sneering at me and looking down her nose at me, like a piece of dirt on the bottom of her shoe. My sister, Mary, said it was because Mother hadn't bonded with me when I was born. If this was the case, at least she could have tried to love me. Personally, I think this is a load of rubbish as there are a number of people who have fostered babies and adopted children. They chose to have these children and they were loved, not hated or treated like I was. Besides, what did my sister know about the early part of my life – she wasn't even there? I was coming up to my twelfth birthday when my sister was born and Mother totally excluded me from family life.

Mother never hit me – it was the names that I was called over the years which hurt. If other children called me names, which they sometimes did, I could shout back at them. But I couldn't shout back at Mother; at least not when I was a child. It was only after I had left home when I was married that I felt able to fight back. If I wet myself Mother would say I was a 'stinky little bastard' and that she wished I was dead. She was always nice to me if other people were about and when my father was there, but when no one was around it was a different story. I was once told that when I lived with Nana Grainger I never soiled myself and I was a happy child. Even when Nana was angry with me or had given me a backhander for doing something wrong, like leaving my brother at the play park when I tore my knickers on the slide, she still loved me. Mother was always calling me a 'fat cow' or a 'dirty pig'. It wasn't my fault that I was overweight – she was the one who fed me.

I learned later on in life that the probable reason why I had wet myself was most likely because of anxiety from all the shouting and the continuous abuse I was subjected to from both of my parents. I now think that Mother knew that my father was sexually abusing me and yet she let it carry on for all those years. Perhaps it was a form of punishment to me for ruining her life. When I wrote the letter to my mother about my father sexually abusing me, she never wanted to talk about it. The last time that I saw her was with her sister, the wicked witch of the west, when she rang on my doorbell in 1985. I have never missed her and was glad that I wrote the letter. Even now Mother still tells people that I was a devious liar and always was. It was usually people I knew whom she told, as Mother always knew that what she said would get back to me. Mother even agreed with Mary that I had probably torn up David's birthday cards when he never received them one year. But my David knew that I wouldn't do something like that.

After a while I found myself looking in the obituaries column of the local paper, hoping that she was dead – the very same thing that she had wished of me. At least then I would have been rid of both of my parents, who as far as I was concerned had taken my childhood away and ruined my life.

I learnt over a period of time, though, that it was better to forgive, in order to be able to move on with my life. Later, when my brother, Johnny, found out from his son, Martin, that Mother had emphysema, Johnny suggested that we should both go to see her to see if we could make peace before it was too late, as Mother was getting on a bit. Johnny and I both went to see her together, so we both witnessed what she said. We thought it best this way as she was known for twisting things around, giving different accounts of the same event to each of us. We had learnt a long time ago that this was always the best policy, especially when Mother was speaking to one but not the other.

We went on a Sunday morning. Johnny knocked on the front door while I stood to one side, where Mother couldn't see me. When she answered the door, she asked him what he wanted. Johnny told her that it was about time that they tried to resolve things. She was about to let him in, when Johnny announced that he had brought me to see her, too. Mother then slammed the door in his face, saying she didn't want to see either of us. But I am sure that if Johnny had been by himself, she would have let him in. When we got back in the car we could see her peeping through the curtains. That was the last time either of us saw or spoke to our mother. Mother still kept up her vendetta with me, though, but I just ignored her abusive words and got on with my life. At least while Mother was running me down, she was leaving some other poor soul alone. Mother forgot that I was well known and that her unkind words would always get back to me.

The Start of it All

When Johnny and I returned to Clacton-on-Sea in Essex after the war, our lives changed completely. Our father had been demobbed from the army and was now working on Clacton Pier as a painter in the winter and as a rides attendant during the summer months.

One of the good times I remember was when he bought a doll for me which we had chosen together. There were two to choose from and I couldn't decide which one to pick: the white one or the black one. Eventually I chose the white one and named her Judy.

Friday night was Dad's night off and he liked to go to the fairground beside Butlins Holiday Camp. He used to save up any tickets he won whilst working at the pier to buy gifts. Our pride and joy were the three-wheel scooters he won – one for each of us.

Dad was a lot harder on Johnny than myself, probably because he was sexually abusing me at the time and so was treating me nicely. I must have been only 3 years old when it first started and I didn't understand what was happening to me. We were living in Birmingham with Nan at the time and he told me it was 'our little secret'. He told me the usual things that abusers are known to say: that if I told anyone I would be taken away and that bad things would happen to me. He also said no one would believe me if I told them. It was only when I was older and understood more that I realised what we were doing was wrong and not normal.

The year 1949 saw one of my worst nightmares as my nan and grandad Chaplin went to Monte Carlo to work for the Mansell family who owned Clacton Pier; my grandad as a chauffeur and Nan as a ladies' maid. It was nice for them but not for me, as they left my father in charge of their house. I cringe at the thought of it even now. Every day he made me go to the house with him, where he continued to have sex with me. You may wonder why I never told anyone when I was older, but I guess I was too frightened of the repercussions. It was at a time when children were 'seen but not heard' and I was one of those children who were too afraid to ask for anything. I was even too scared to ask anyone if I could go to the toilet. I always had wet knickers unless I was in my own home or at Nan's and this continued even when I went to senior school.

As well as Olive Palmer – now Olive Pierson after she married and went to live in the USA, whom I still keep in touch with – one of my other best friends was Barbara Cooper, who passed away at the age of 21 with a brain tumour. I still keep in touch with Barbara's sister, Margaret. We weren't supposed to play with her as they were classed as a 'scruffy family', but Olive and I liked her. We also felt sorry for her as her father was always hitting her around the head, especially after he had been on the drink.

Our parents always knew when we had been together as my grandad Chaplin used to cut my hair. My grandad's brothers were taught the trade and they all had barbers shops in and around Colchester. Anyway, one day after school he cut my hair and found that it was full of nits. Down went the scissors and he went straight round to tell Aunt Nell, Olive's mum, on the assumption she would have them, too. Poor Olive had lovely long hair and Aunt Nell told Grandad to cut it really short. She cried and cried, but we were told it was our own fault for playing with Barbara. It didn't make a lot of difference though, as we still played with her.

We all went to St Osyth Road School, where my brother also started. After three days the attendance officer went to see my mother to find out why my brother hadn't started and it turned out that he had been there all along but they had been calling him David Granger; he had always been called Johnny Granger at home and hadn't put two and two together that it was him they were referring to when they called the register.

Olive and I spent lots of time at the swimming pool on Clacton Pier. We used to tell the man on the gate that we wanted to see my dad and so got onto the pier for nothing. Then we used to find Dad, who used to get us into the pool area. We spent all day there and it backed onto a cafe. At lunchtime he used to buy us something to eat. It was great in those days as we used to have lots of hot summers.

We both loved school on Mondays as Nan used to make lovely curries from Sunday's leftover joint of meat, potatoes and butter beans. We used to run home that day because we knew she would always save us some. Olive still talks about it when we talk on the phone today. We used to play games like chase, hop scotch, truth or dare, love and promise, ball games, skipping and lots more. In fact, we used to get up to all sorts of mischief, including one occasion when we chased poor Barbara up the road screaming. We each had a chicken leg in our hands which Grandad had given us and if you pulled the tendons it would move.

The year 1950 was the last year at junior school and I started at Pathfield Road Senior School in the September. My sister was born on 26 July 1950 and we named her Sandra after a school friend of mine. She never liked her name and later she changed it to Katie by deed poll when she moved to London.

The year 1950 is another year that haunts me. In the 1950s there were no hospitals nearby that had birthing units, so my sister was born in a large house, next to the health clinic, called a maternity home. When my mother went into the maternity home in Clacton, my father made me sleep in his bed where the inevitable used to happen. He used to make sure I was back in my own bed before my brother woke up as we both slept in the same room. There were only two bedrooms and there wasn't enough room for two single beds in the room, so we used to sleep on camp beds. Sometimes I managed to get Olive's mum and dad (Aunt Nell and Uncle George) to let me stay with them for a couple of nights to get away from him.

A few weeks after my mother and sister came home we moved to our first council house at 76 North Road in Great Clacton, where I lived for most of my life until I married in 1960. It had three bedrooms and a bathroom; we didn't have a bathroom in Dudley Road and had to bathe in a tin one in front of the fire.

My sister was about three months old when she was taken to Clacton Hospital with a large lump on her head. It turned out to be a tumour and she was operated on straight away. She was lucky that they had caught it in time and she survived the operation. I had started at senior school by this time and hurried home each day to see if Sandra had come home. Then one afternoon Mother came to meet me and she had my baby sister with her.

Olive had started senior school a year earlier, being a year older. I met new school friends but we still went round together after school and during the holidays. My best friend at senior school was a girl called Sheila Denney. We sat together in class and were always getting up to mischief. I remember one day when I had a spring rash and Sheila had put her hand up and told the maths teacher that I had spots like the measles. He came over, lifted up my sleeve with a ruler and then sent me to the head master, who sent me home; though we both knew it was a rash as I often got them. My mother asked why they had sent me home and I told her the school said that I had to go to the doctor. I was taken that evening and I was given a couple of weeks off school.

I hated sports, especially hockey, so I used to make sure I caught the teacher on the ankle with the hockey stock so I got sent off. One day in art class I asked if I could go to the toilet but the teacher refused to let me go. I gave her some cheek and she locked me in the art cupboard where all the paint and art materials were stored. I thought I'd teach her a lesson, so I found a jar in the cupboard, spent a penny in it and then left it on the shelf.

On another occasion the class were taken on a trip – first to the waterworks and then on to the gasworks. In those days we had to walk. I managed to keep up as far as the waterworks, but was lagging behind a bit thereafter. The teacher shouted at me and I was sent back to school. I was on my way back when one of the men who worked at the waterworks stopped his van and asked what was wrong as he had seen me on the tour round the waterworks earlier. I told him what the teacher had said, so he told me to jump in the van and I arrived at the gasworks before the rest of the class. When the teacher saw me, she asked why I wasn't back at school and how I had got there. Not thinking about it, I shouted back at her, 'How do you think? I grew wings and flew,' flapping my arms about like a bird. The teacher gave me a slap around the head with a rolled-up paper for my cheek and I also got a detention after school for my pains.

In Denial

It started when I was 3 years old with my father touching and licking my vagina. I didn't feel anything at that age and thought it was normal.

I was ten before he penetrated me and came inside me for the first time in 1949, when he was looking after my grandparents' house as they were away in France. It was on my nan and granddad Chaplin's bed and I had to go there every day with him, where he would make me take my knickers off. The first time it happened was really horrible as it hurt and I bled. He'd even put a towel underneath me so that I didn't make a mess on the bed. Later, he put it in the wash basket for my mother to wash. Mother never queried it and neither did she when I put wet knickers in there, but she must have known. Sometimes he would take me from the front and other times he would make me go down on my knees and take me from behind. I never said anything because my mother would have said I was a liar. It was only when my sister spoke up that he'd tried it once with her that my mother could no longer deny it.

My mother and I never had a close relationship and never talked about the birds and bees. I learnt about how you got pregnant at school. When I was eleven I started my periods, at which point he was careful and used condoms until I got married. A year after I married, I had Edward.

It was when I learnt about sex at school, at the age of 10 or 11, that I first realised it was wrong. Whilst I was horrified and I felt sick at the time, I was still too frightened to speak out. It was awful. I felt it was my fault as well and that I had somehow contributed to it – that it was just as much me as him. I got to that age where you feel shame and yet didn't know what to do, so I used to put it to the back of my mind until I was on my own with him again, living the nightmare.

When we lived at the flat my brother, Johnny, was in the same room as me, so my father never visited my bedroom. It was my only place of sanctity. It was only when my mother was away at the maternity home that he made me sleep in his room, when I was aged between 10 and 11, when my sister was born. He used to wait for me to come home from work and when Mother went to bed early, he would have me up against the wall between the living room and the hall. But that wasn't as bad as when he used to take me in the churchyard on our way back from the fish and chip shop.

Every Friday night my father and I used to cycle down to the shops to get fish and chips. My sister used to want to come with us on her bike, but my father never used to let her as she couldn't ride a bike as she was too small and it would have meant we'd have to walk. My mother always agreed with him and I'm sure she must have known what he was doing to me as she used to scrub the kitchen floor every Friday night when we were gone. It didn't take long to go to the chip shop on bikes and she never questioned the fact that we were gone for ages. We used to cut through from Valley Road, where we turned off and went past some fields into the churchyard, where he would have his wicked way with me. Even now, I still can't visit the churchyard and it makes me cringe every time we go past it.

Sometimes he'd make me masturbate him. This was usually when he was unable to have sex with me as I was menstruating.

When I was 13 years old, he told me that if I ever wanted sex, I should go to him and that I wasn't to have it with anyone else. I did not have any other sexual contact until I had an affair with my aunt's husband when I was living in Scotland at the age of 16 years old. Even Neville, my first husband, knew nothing about it, even after it all came out; although, David knew because I had spoken to him.

My father didn't drink because he didn't believe in it. Neither did he believe in gambling. His own father was a drunk and abusive to him, which might have had something to do with it, although I don't know in what way as no one ever talked about anything like that in those days. I later discovered that he came from a community which practised incest.

As a child, I always used to have wet knickers. I was usually fine when I was away elsewhere at a friend's or at school because he wasn't around, but the moment I got home I would wet myself. It was always daytime wetting out of fear and it started when I was very small. If I was out at someone's house I was too frightened to ask anyone to go to the toilet. One of my friends had an outside toilet and it was dark, which might have had something to do with it, as I used to wait until I got home, by which time I would have wet knickers, although I suspect it was more to do with my father. But I was fine in school and no one ever picked up on the fact that I was being abused. I was a very quiet child and wouldn't say anything to anyone. It was only when I wrote a letter to my mother years later that anyone knew.

I was fine if I came home and someone else was in the house, as he wouldn't do anything when Mother was actually about – only when she had gone to bed and there was no one else there. I used to feel relief whenever I got home from work when others were in the house, as it meant I didn't have to worry about whether or not he was going to make a move on me. But if the house was empty, I knew what was going to happen – it was just a question of when. It felt horrid and dirty. All I could do was wash and scrub myself afterwards, but it still never got rid of it – at least not in my mind. I couldn't speak out and it was only when I saw a counsellor when a doctor had sent me there following a bout of depression that I could finally speak about what had happened.

I used to try to nip out if I knew I was alone in the house, but he used to catch me between the living room and the stairs. He used to call out to me saying that he wanted me for a minute and then he used to stop me from going upstairs. I knew then that that was it and he would be behind me moments later. He used to say, 'I love you, you know I love you.' But it was the wrong sort of love.

Once I knew it was wrong I was fearful of the repercussions. It didn't enter my head that he might go to prison.

Whenever something about sex came on the television, I used to have to turn it off; otherwise, I knew he'd be coming for me. Even now, I don't like reading books or watching television if it refers to sexual scenes, but I do like to read books about children who have gone through the same as I have – some worse than myself – as it makes me realise that I wasn't on my own. Any news that involves child abuse makes me think of my father. This is a wicked world and seems to get worse. The only difference now is that people are more open about things than they were in the sixties and before that. I have not had any sexual contact with any of my husbands – only when my first husband pestered me. With Geoffrey it was one of the reasons our marriage was annulled. David never bothered me unless I felt like it. I was fine with David as I love him and the sexual side is part of a marriage. I sometimes wish I had not had my tubes cut and sewn, as when David and I married we could have had another child together. It would not have replaced Jeremy, but could have helped me to recover more quickly after his passing. I would never recommend anyone undergoing any type of surgery like I did – if I hadn't had it, I might have had that chance to have another child.

You can put things to the back of your mind, but there is always something that will trigger it off – and usually when you least expect it. You can forgive someone for their actions of abuse, but you can never forget ...

My Sister

My sister, Sandra, was quite clever and was able to do jigsaw puzzles at the age of nine months. I loved her very much and desperately wanted to protect her from my father. As I became older, I used to take her everywhere I could. Sandra was spoilt by both myself and our brother, Johnny; especially Johnny. On a couple of occasions I took Sandra with me on holiday, once to Birmingham and once to Yarmouth. I didn't want Sandra left at home in Father's clutches. Maybe he wouldn't have touched her, but I didn't want to leave it to chance. I don't remember Sandra having many friends, either at school or when she was in her teenage years. But two people in particular still come to mind. One was a school friend whom she had sleepovers with called Diane, who was 13 years old. She lived just around the corner and they were always together. I was watching the evening news on television one night, when Diane's picture was shown on the screen and the newscaster announced that she had been hit by a car and killed. I don't know how Sandra felt at the time as she was just a child herself, but it must have had some impact as they spent a lot of time together. I was told that Diane and her brother had been out carol singing and were crossing the road, when Diane was hit by a car, killing her instantly.

Sandra then became friends with another young girl, whose name I cannot recall. For the purposes of this book, I will call her Susan. Sandra and Susan were in their teens and were still at school. It was during the flower power age, when people did scatty things like chasing rock bands all over different towns. Sandra and Susan were often playing truant from school, hitch-hiking everywhere to see the bands they were interested in. On one of these occasions, my father had to go to London as Sandra was being held on a drugs charge and was to appear at the Old Bailey. Sandra wouldn't tell the police what the pills were, so they were confiscated for tests, proving they were prescription drugs for Sandra's asthma. Sandra was then taken home by Father, who was not best pleased, having had to take time off work.

Sandra remained friendly with Susan afterwards and they still did daft things together until tragedy struck, when Sandra heard that Susan had committed suicide, after losing another friend. Sandra never bothered to have a close friendship with anyone else after that.

I didn't have a lot of contact with Sandra as she got older. Sandra had wasted a lot of her time skipping school and she had no qualifications, so she enrolled at college to take a course in childcare and nursery nursing. She was desperate to work with children and she studied hard to pass the exams, later moving to London to work. I never saw my sister again after that. At the time, Mother and I didn't have a lot of communication and we were always falling out with each other. It was when I was married to Geoffrey that I heard that Mother and Sandra were telling people that I had married Geoffrey for his money; it was mainly Mother spreading the gossip, as usual. Geoffrey didn't have money, but he owned his own house which had been left to him by his mother. Geoffrey had also bought a new car, so presumably that's how Mother came to the conclusion that he had plenty of money.

I didn't hear any news about my sister until several years later, when out of the blue I had a phone call from Mother. It was Easter, but I cannot remember the year. The call was to tell me Sandra had given birth to a baby girl, Pippa, on 6 April. Mother had known about the pregnancy but had been forced not to tell anyone, or so she said. Sandra wasn't sure if she would keep the baby as it had water on the brain and so would have disabilities. Mother asked if I would knit some baby clothes for her as the ones Sandra had bought were too big. I said that I would and that if she gave me Sandra's address I would post them to her. Mother said she couldn't give me the address as Sandra didn't want me to know. Instead, she agreed to meet me when I had finished them and said that she would deliver them to Sandra herself. Like the idiot I was, I agreed to do it, but I felt hurt that my sister didn't want me to contact her. To this day I wonder whether it was really my sister's wishes or if it was Mother trying to keep me and Sandra apart. Anyway, at the time I didn't want to rock the boat, as the saying goes, and so didn't ask any questions. Mother and I didn't really talk to each other when I handed the clothes over. I had to be careful what I said in her company, in case it turned into an argument. I don't really know what was exchanged between them, but Mother would often tell me one story and my siblings another, so one never knew what to believe anyway.

A few years later, when I was working for a fish shop, on my day off which was on a Monday, I used to travel by train to see my sister and her daughter, Pippa. My husband, Geoffrey, worked on the railway, so it didn't cost me anything to travel to London. One day I was sitting at the table with Pippa playing with her. Sandra wasn't exactly a tidy person and I had to move some books to one side so I could clear the table. On top of the pile was Sandra's diary, which was open. I picked it up to close it and staring at me was something that she had written: that I used Mother's place like a hotel, took advantage of her. It must have been around the time that Johnny had asked Mother if I could stay with her when I was having driving lessons with him. I was going to take my driving test at Clacton, where Mother was living at the time. It was the only time I had stayed at Mother's since we'd lived together as a family. I was invited to stay for Christmas, the year my daughter Mary was born.

I thought at the time how two-faced my sister was. I was very careful what I said to her in future. Sandra and I gradually grew apart; though, I visited her occasionally after she was married and had moved to a larger house. Sandra had four children – three girls and a boy. I can no longer remember their names, only Pippa. We still kept in touch whenever Sandra visited my mother on her annual holiday, but it was only a flying visit – half an hour if I was lucky. The last time we had contact was at Mother's funeral and we haven't seen each other since.

Scottish Horizons

When I was fourteen I wanted to get a Saturday job serving in a shop, so I went to Woolworths in Clacton to see the manager. He was a little man not much taller than myself called Mr Griffiths. He was a nice person and said, 'You're not very tall, but we can always stand you on a box if you can't reach the counter.' He then took me to see the head supervisor, who took my details and said I was to start on Saturday afternoon at 1.30 p.m.

I earned six shillings for each afternoon and £1.1s. when we worked all week during the school holidays. My parents let me buy my first bike on the never-never, making weekly payments until it was paid for, but most of my money was spent on my little sister. I used to get her a dress nearly every week, as I liked to see her looking nice whenever I took her out.

Whenever anyone new started they had to work on each counter so they could learn about different things. It was not like today, where the tills add up for you; we had to add up in our head. I got on well with everyone and I was very happy there. I remember one summer when I was on the ice cream and sundae counter and I had to get an ice cream out of the freezer. It was very deep and the ice cream was right at the bottom. As I leaned over I fell in and all you could see were my legs and feet sticking out, by all accounts. The supervisor was called but instead of getting me out straight away, he went to fetch the manager. Everybody was laughing. I could always see the funny side of things and their laughter inevitably set me off, which made everybody worse as I have a wicked laugh which makes people laugh even more.

When I was about fourteen my nan and grandad moved to Colchester so Grandad Chaplin could be nearer to his job. Sometimes on my day off I would cycle to their new home to visit them, but when my sister got older I used to go on the bus with her; I used to take her out everywhere with me to protect her from my father. Grandad used to wait at the top of Clingo Hill for our bus and when we saw his car we would get off at Greenstead Road Post Office and climb into the car to travel the rest of the way with him.

When I left school at fifteen I stayed on at Woolworths and was put in charge of the toy counter, where we were responsible for ordering our own stock for downstairs as well as the stockroom upstairs. But my troubles began the year I was fifteen, when I went to Scotland to see my Aunt Joanne for a holiday. The holiday was good, but a few days before I came home my Uncle William started to make advances towards me. I didn't mind initially as I had become infatuated by him – I suppose at the time I thought it was love. He wanted me to go back and live with them and I said that I would love to but that I didn't think my parents would allow me to. I don't know the contents of the letter, but my aunt wrote to my parents. I don't think she would have done so had she known what was going to happen, though.

I asked my boss at Woolworths if it was possible to get a transfer up to Scotland and he said he would arrange it with the store in question. He said he would be sorry to lose me but if things didn't work out I could always have my old job back.

Just before Christmas the same year my dear Grandad was taken into hospital in London and was diagnosed with cancer. Gran, Dad and myself used to go by train on a Sunday to visit him. The last I saw of him was on his birthday on 31 December 1954. Sadly, he passed away the following week on 6 January 1955. I had lost someone who was very dear to me.

My aunt came down from Scotland for the funeral and she wanted to take me back with her. I asked my manager if the transfer could be rushed through and he was kind enough to oblige. I remember saying goodbye to him and the head supervisor, Mrs Davey. A couple of days later I was on my way to Ayrshire in Scotland to be with my aunt and uncle. They lived in a house that belonged to the farmer they worked for. My uncle was a dairy man and my aunt washed the milk churns in the dairy. On my first day in Scotland I went into Ayrshire to report to the Woolworths store where I was going to work and I started the next day.

I was getting on quite well when, on 3 February, I was rushed into hospital with appendicitis. The hospital was 18 miles away and I had to go on my own. In the early hours of the morning the hospital rang the farm and asked if the farmer could get my uncle on the phone as they needed permission to operate as I was under sixteen.

After the operation I was told that I was very lucky, as when they opened me up they discovered that it had been about to burst. I was very ill for a couple of days but soon began to pick up. My aunt came and visited only once as it was a long way away, but I didn't mind as I made friends easily wherever I went. The patients on my ward were all very friendly and we all liked a good laugh. I was always getting told off for making them laugh as it made our temperatures go up and then we couldn't go home.

I remember one morning on the rounds we were asked if we had been to the toilet. I hadn't been since my operation, so the sister left instructions that I was to be given something to make me go. The patient on my right said that it was awful stuff and that she didn't envy me. Well, I hate taking medicine at the best of times, so I wondered how I was going to get out of it. The patient on my left was half asleep when they came round with the medicine, so when the nurse asked who it was for, I told her that it was for the patient on my left and she gave it to her instead. Needless to say, I made sure that by the next day I had been. In fact, I stopped in the loo for two hours until I had been. The lady who had the medicine couldn't understand how she had got the trots all of a sudden and put it down to something she'd eaten. I couldn't keep a straight face and started to laugh, which made all the others laugh, including the poor woman who had taken my medicine; I was never brave enough to own up and none of the others said anything, either.

When I went home, William and Joanne told me they were going to move to another job so I had to give in my notice at Woolworths to move with them. We moved to a little island across the water from Greenock, which is where our affair began, but not right away. I applied to the local Woolworths and was given a job there, but it was tiring as I had to get up early each morning and walk 2 miles to catch the ferry across to Greenock. If I was lucky and got out from work on time, I was able to get a bus in time to catch the six o'clock ferry, which would enable me to get a connection for the bus to the cove. If I missed it I would have to wait for the seven o'clock ferry and walk the rest of the way, which made it a long day.

My affair with William started a few weeks after we moved to the cove. I can't remember exactly when it was, only that Joanne and I'd had a row and thought that I should return home to Clacton. William was against this and Joanne threw a cup at me, catching me on the top of my eye. It left quite a deep cut and a scar which is still visible today. I don't know what happened between them after that, but she left the house and took the children with her. We discovered later that they had gone back to England to see my parents, to tell them about the affair and to see if there was any way that the police could bring me back, but under the Scottish law they couldn't do anything as I was now sixteen.

After she had left I had to leave my job and work in the dairy, where I learnt to milk the cows and clean the milk churns. Joanne returned to Scotland shortly after but went to live a refuge in Glasgow. William and I went to fetch her home, to make a new start, and a few weeks later we were on the move again to another job they had taken in a place called Dalkeith, near to the City of Edinburgh. By now I wasn't working, so I wrote home to see if my parents would send me some money for the train fare home, as I couldn't expect my aunt and uncle to pay my way. I left on a hot and sunny afternoon in August while William and Joanne were at work. I was going back home, although I wasn't looking forward to it as I knew I was returning to more abuse.

My First Proper Relationship

Nothing was ever mentioned about what had happened in Scotland. I was glad as I knew it was wrong and sincerely wished it had never happened. I went back to Woolworths to see if I could get my old job back and they put me on the household counter selling soap powder and various cleaning products. I got friendly with a girl called Jean Oliver, who was married to Alex who owned a fish and chip shop. One Sunday they took me to see Jean's parents and family, who lived not far from Layer Crossroads in Colchester. They were a nice family and Jean's brother, Hurbert, otherwise known as Bert, became my first proper boyfriend.

Bert was a lot older than myself and he was an attentive, considerate person. He never made any advances towards me and was always kind. He wasn't very good-looking, as he only had one eye – he lost the other one in a motorbike accident – but in my experience it's not what people look like, it's what they are like as a person. He was a good man and I liked him very much. Now I had a boyfriend, I thought my father would leave me alone, but he didn't, he only got worse. I still don't know why I didn't speak up, but I guess it was because I was still afraid of him.

My father didn't like me going out with Bert as he said he was too old for me, but I took no notice. One Sunday morning Bert turned up with a tandem bike. He had bought it so we could ride over to his parents' for the day every Sunday. He used to ride to my house each week and together we would ride back to his parents' house. After tea we would have to make our way back to Clacton. He would then make his way home again on the bike. It was bad enough cycling two ways, but to do it twice in one day showed how keen he was.

I stayed with Bert until October, when my father decided to change his job to go and work at the brickworks in Birmingham. I thought at last I would be able to have a normal life and be free of him while he was away, but unfortunately my parents said I had to go with them and once again I left my job at Woolworths. I wasn't happy about it though, as I knew the abuse would continue whenever he got the chance.

We went to stay at Foxwell Road with my nan, my aunt Daisy (who was now married), my uncle Jack and two cousins, Lynne and Colin. Lynne was blind, but this wasn't discovered until she was 9 months old. I managed to get a job in the city centre not far from the Bull Ring shopping centre working in a dry-cleaners. I liked my job and got on well with the staff there. There were only a five of us plus the manager and we had quite a lot of laughs while I was there.

When it came to Christmas all the branches of the shop got together for a works party at quite a posh place. There was a fair few of us all and the evening was going well until we were served with our Christmas pudding, when I happened to look across the table at the girl opposite me. The lens had fallen out of one side of her glasses into her custard and with my sense of humour I couldn't keep a straight face. Anyway, I started laughing and set everyone else off. When I finally managed to stop laughing, they asked me what was so funny. I tried to tell them but it only started me off again. Eventually, I managed to spit the story out between gales of laughter. The poor girl hadn't even noticed, but by this time she was laughing as well. Apparently, I had made their night, but goodness knows how she had never noticed.

By the time we returned to Great Clacton I was about eighteen and once again I went back to my old job at Woolworths. I was given a position in the stockroom stacking shelves as well as my own aisles to look after and I liked it. We had to use a ladder to get to the top bins and sometimes we had to sit on the top bin to hang things from the ceiling. Occasionally, on a Saturday, Mr Griffiths, the manager would bring his two young sons into work and he would send them up to the stockroom so I could look after them and they would help me unpack the stock.

On one particular Saturday I had to climb on the top bin to hang tin kettles on the ceiling. One of the boys was passing me the kettles, but while I was hanging them the eldest one took the ladder away and left me up there for about an hour. They were lovely boys, though, and we used to have a lot of fun.

One year when we had our Christmas party we played lots of games. Mr Griffiths was in charge and he requested that all the girls who wore size 4 shoes should step forwards. There were five of us, including myself. He then announced that whoever danced the cancan best would win some sandals. The others all vanished and left me standing, so I just carried on dancing as they played the music faster and faster until I fell on the floor with my legs in the air and my knickers showing. Needless to say, I won the sandals and gave them a good laugh at the same time.

I made friends with one of the girls at work, Jean Gibbs and we often travelled into Colchester on a Saturday evening as there wasn't much to do in Clacton, especially during the winter. We usually went to a little pub called The Robin Hood, which wasn't far from the bus station. One evening while we were there, Jean met a young man called Jim Hussey and they became an item. The following Saturday I offered to stay at home as it wasn't fair on them to have me tagging along playing gooseberry. When Jean came into work on the Monday, she said that Jim had a mate who wanted to meet me and she had arranged a blind date for the next Saturday evening.

The following Saturday Jean and I went into Colchester to meet Jim and my blind date, Neville. They had arranged to meet at the milk bar opposite the bus station in St John's Street. Jim hung around near the door to keep a lookout for him and eventually he told me he was coming. When he entered the milk bar all I could see was this bloke with a long nose and a bunch of flowers.

We started to go out together, although I wasn't that keen on him. We used to go out as a foursome and we had lots of happy and amusing times together. One Sunday we went to Dedham and took a rowing boat out onto the river. It was OK until I spotted some fish floating on the surface of the water. Not liking dead things I panicked, rocked the boat and fell in. I was soaked from head to foot and Jean and I still had to catch the last bus back to Clacton. We all decided that we would walk back to the village together so we could catch the bus, but we got lost and it took us ages to get there. We only just made it in time to catch the last bus into Colchester and we had to run to catch the last connection to Clacton.

When I first met Neville he lived with his parents and worked on a farm just off Severalls Lane in Colchester. It was a long walk to get there as the buses didn't go along their lane. When I got to know him a bit better I felt sorry for him, as I found out that his mother and sister took most of his wages off him. The first time I went to stay at his house for the weekend I had the shock of my life as their huge Dalmatian stole my knickers off the line and wouldn't give them back.

Neville and I dated on and off until I was twenty-one. All the time I was hoping my father would leave me alone, but he didn't. I was never intimate with Neville as I hated the idea of it, although it didn't stop him from pestering me. Each time I would put him off, saying I wanted to wait until I got married.

Just after my twenty-first birthday we decided to get married. I didn't love him but I needed to get away from home. We talked about it at the weekend and on the Monday, without telling anyone, Neville went to the registry office to arrange for a special licence to get married the following Saturday, 26 March 1960. He came to see me that evening and it was all arranged for one o'clock. I was sure he'd got it wrong, as it closed at 12.30 p.m. on a Saturday, and so I sent him back the next day to check. They wrote the details down on a piece of paper for him and it turned out that he was right. Because the end of the tax year was coming up, the office stayed open longer for the last few weeks of each tax year.

That night we told our respective parents and none of them were very happy with the arrangement, but they couldn't do anything about it as we were both old enough to make up our own minds. Neville was now living in Elmstead Market with his family. Neville's brother, Derek, lived down the lane not far from him. He was married to Evelyn and they had a little girl, although I can't remember her name. Derek and Evelyn were very nice and I always enjoyed visiting them.

The week we were to get married they told me that Neville couldn't read and write, so the rest of that week I had to teach him to write his name. I knew nothing about Neville until we had informed our parents the Monday before we were to be married, which is when Neville's sister-in-law told me about Neville's illiteracy. I had never suspected a thing and he had kept it well hidden during the course of our relationship of about three years. I used to stay over at his parents' house and nothing was ever said about it. His sister was educated and even she didn't say anything. His brother, Derek, was also unable to read and write and if he went shopping he used to carry pictures around with him; he also passed his driving test this way, using pictures. He used to draw them himself so he knew what he was getting. For instance, he would draw a block of butter or a milk bottle. I guess I didn't really even think about it at the time as my priority was just getting away from home and Neville gave me that opportunity, even though the abuse from my father continued.

Apparently, they had been kept at home to do household chores and their parents were never in a job or at the same address long enough for the education authority to catch up with them. Neville left the job where he worked the same weekend we were married and got another one at Colchester Corporation on the dustcarts. Neville's parents and sister didn't want to come to the wedding but Derek, Evelyn and the baby would be there, so it was arranged that we would all meet up on the bus to Colchester.

The Monday before the wedding I asked if I could have the Saturday off work to get married, but Mrs Davey didn't believe me, so she went round to ask my mother, who was working in the store at that time and continued to do so until her retirement. Mother was given the day off as well and the staff had a collection and bought us a lovely cutlery set for our wedding present.

On the Friday night before the wedding I advised Neville to come straight round to mine after work and give me his wages for safe-keeping, so that his mother didn't take them off him, which he did. But when Neville went home that night they had thrown all his stuff out and so he had to go to his brother's to sleep.

All my family were there and it was the longest ceremony ever held in history in a registry office. Instead of the normal time it took an hour, because Neville couldn't say 'lawful' and kept saying 'awful'. In the end, the registrar split the word into two parts, so he could say 'law' and then 'ful'. The next couple who were waiting asked if it was a wedding, a birth and a funeral all rolled into one as we had taken so long to say our vows. They also weren't a very happy couple as they had now lost their train connections to wherever it was they were going for their honeymoon.

After the wedding we all went back to Clacton, where my family laid on a lavish spread and a wedding cake. We left at about nine o'clock that night for Colchester. Neville had arranged a bedsit for us to stay in that week. It so happened that we got off the bus just as Neville's parents were waiting to get on, but they just ignored us, certain that we had only got married because I was pregnant. What they didn't know was that it wasn't me who was pregnant but Neville's sister ...

The Early Years

Neville and I spent our first night in a bedsit in Military Road in Colchester. The door to the room had two holes in it and so I had to cover them up with a coat as someone kept looking through them. It turned out to be the landlady's son. The following morning I sent Neville to Clacton to collect some china which I had left at my former home. While he was gone the landlady came to see me to say that she was sorry about her son but that he was a little backward. Then she told me that Neville and I could move into the caravan in her garden if we wanted more privacy, which was about four doors down. By the time Neville got back I had already moved our stuff and was busy cooking our first Sunday lunch.

It was quite cosy in the caravan and at least we now had our own space. I continued to travel to Clacton to work, leaving home early to catch the eight o'clock bus and returning at about 7.30 p.m. It was a long, tiring day, so later that year I decided to get a job on the corporation buses as a conductress, where my brother was already working as a driver.

I applied for my licence and I was soon on my way. I was taken on the various routes with another conductress called Ruby, who later became my next-door neighbour. I learned the ropes very quickly and in less than a fortnight I was on my own. I enjoyed working on the buses and got to know a lot of the regular passengers. We also had lots of laughs.

Before St Boltophs area was altered and Queen Street was made a one-way system, there used to be a bus stop just before you turned into St John Street outside a paper shop. One day, I stopped to let some passengers off and to help a lady off with her pushchair. I was just helping her collapse the pushchair, when all of a sudden the bus drove off before I could climb back on. I had to run all the way to the next stop, which was near the arcade, and was quite a way away. The driver was waiting for me as a passenger had gone round to the front of the bus to tell him he had left me behind. Apparently, someone had rung the bell and he had assumed it was me. In those days the buses had open-end platforms at the back while the driver's cab was in the front, obscured from view. I used to climb up on the front of this platform to turn the handle to change the destination on the route.

I didn't have much of a sexual relationship with Neville as I hated that side of married life owing to my experiences with my father. I realise that this was unfair on Neville, but that was the way I felt. My father was still at it, even though I was married, and he used to come up to see me, usually when Neville wasn't there. To this day I still don't know why I never spoke about what was going on. It was probably because I was ashamed that it was happening and because my mother always denied that anything was going on. I had written letters to both my mother and sister and I was told by my uncle Henry – the youngest of Nan Chaplin's children – months ago that Mother did know about the sexual abuse but chose not to do anything about it. My parents were always fighting and arguing, so by letting it continue, it stopped him from pestering her. Now, I realise my mum was as much to blame as my father.

After a few months we moved from the caravan into a bedsit in Mersea Road, opposite Meyrick Road, as the caravan was too damp during the winter. Our new landlords were very nice people and we stayed with them until we got our first flat in Wellesley Road nearer to the town centre. Later that year I fell pregnant with my first child, who was born the following year. I am not sure whether or not the baby was Neville's, as we hadn't been sleeping together that way, and so I'm relatively sure that it was my father's, as he was still coming to the flat on my days off to do some decorating for us and the inevitable usually happened. I kept this secret for years and Neville never worked it out. As I said before, he was unable to read or write and was a little backward. It wasn't his fault, as he hadn't had an education because his parents were always moving from place to place and as I already said, the boys were kept at home to help out. The only good thing about getting pregnant was that my father never touched me again.

I was still working on the buses and left a month before the baby was born. With only four weeks to go before the baby was due, my sister, Sandra, came to stay with me for the Easter holidays after she had broken up from school. On the first Monday she was with us I had to take her to see my doctor who lived at the end of our road as she had developed a rash. It turned out that she had caught German measles. Apparently, she had caught it off her friend who had been off school with the same thing. My parents knew about this but had omitted to tell me. Fortunately, the doctor said I would be all right as I had passed the three-month stage, where I was unlikely to have anything wrong with my baby. The doctor said if I was going to catch it, it had better be soon or I would be unable to go into the maternity home.

My sister went home the following Friday as I wasn't feeling too well and on the Saturday morning I had to call out the doctor as I was covered from head to foot with a rash from German measles. I was very ill with it and was bedridden. The doctor visited me every day until I was well enough to get back on my feet.

A week later I had to go for a check-up. The doctor was a bit concerned about the baby and so he sent me to the hospital for a scan. I went back to the surgery the next morning to get my results and was told that I was being admitted to the maternity home straight away and that they were expecting me. As Neville was at work I left a message with my nan Chaplin, as I knew that he would go over there if I wasn't at home. It was no good leaving him a note as he was unable to read it.

I stayed at the maternity home for the rest of the week. In the meantime my own doctor had retired and so I registered with another, who was very nice and helped me a lot over the following years. He came to see me in the maternity wing and they said they were going to induce me to bring the labour on.

Nothing happened that day and so on the Tuesday they decided they would start me off on a drip. By one o'clock the pains had started and I was taken down to the labour ward. Neville came in later to see me but wouldn't stay. When he went round to Nan's that night he told her I was lying there with a broken arm, which worried her. He didn't know much about anything and assumed it was broken because my arm was strapped to a splint, which was actually a drip to start the labour off.

I had a hard time during my labour and they were about to give me a caesarean because it was a face presentation, when the head started to show. When the contractions started I was moved to the delivery room and at 7.30 p.m. on 29 May 1962 Edward Andrew emerged into the world, a couple of days before his due date. It was a difficult birth and he was taken straight down to be put in an incubator, rather than being placed in my arms.

The next day I asked the sister in charge why I hadn't seen my baby and she explained that he had something wrong with him but didn't say what. The first thing I thought was that he had one leg longer than the other or some sort of disability. But it was the way she was holding him when she returned a short while later that I realised he was fine. 'He's just like Hoppity, the little boy on television,' I cried.

He had been put in an incubator because the features on his face had been squashed during the delivery with it having been a face presentation, but fortunately he was OK. He had a full head of jet black hair and he weighed 5 lb 3 oz. He was classed as premature as he was supposed to have been born around 2 June.

At the time we were living at 30 Wellesley Road in Colchester. Later, we moved to the upstairs flat, as the lady who owned the property was coming back from abroad and wanted to have the downstairs flat altered so that she could move back in herself. We got on very well and she let me put Edward out in her front garden where she could keep an eye on him.

Edward was the worst one out of my children for sleeping at night. He needed feeding every two hours and as I couldn't feed him myself, I had to get up to make his bottles each time. I had tried to breastfeed but he was too lazy to hold on and suck.

Then nine months after Edward was born I fell pregnant with my second child, Mary, who was due on 3 December 1963. I received a letter in late November from the housing department, informing me that they had a house for me and if I was interested, I could pick up the keys the following Thursday, 3 December – the same day the baby was due. The reason the letter was sent to me was because the council knew from when we had registered on the housing waiting list that Neville was unable to read and could only write his name. Neville went with me and when the housing officer learnt that I was due that day, she laughed and said I had better get going, in case I gave birth there and then. Neville and I had been to see the property and we agreed to take it. Neville paid the rent and was given the keys to the house that day. It was a brand-new three-bedroomed house on the Greenstead Estate. The following Monday we both moved into our new home and Nan moved in with us for a while as she was going to look after Edward while I was in the nursing home.

A week later on the Monday morning I had to call the doctor out for Edward as he was very chesty and was struggling to breathe. He gave me a prescription but the nearest chemist was just past East Gates, so I caught a bus. But when I got there they were unable to do it. I didn't know when the next bus was due, so I decided to walk up the hill to the town, which was tiring, especially considering I was heavily pregnant.

That night, as I was watching *Coronation Street* on the television, my labour pains started. I waited until nine o'clock before saying anything to Neville, then I asked him to go to the phone box and dial for an ambulance. At first he started to panic and said that he didn't know how to use the phone. Nan didn't know either, so I had to knock on the neighbour's door. They had only just moved in themselves and the man phoned for me while his wife, Jean, stayed with me until the ambulance arrived. I went by myself, as I knew that Neville would be useless.

On arrival I was admitted straight away and went through the usual procedure. After I had been examined the nurse was really nasty to me and said that I was nowhere near ready to have the baby and that I would have to go home the next day. But at twenty past one in the early hours of Tuesday morning on 10 December I had to ring the bell as I was in such pain that I couldn't move. The sister came in and walked me down to the labour ward. I had one leg on the delivery table, when my waters broke, and a few seconds later, at 1.40 a.m., Mary Jane was born weighing 6 lb 8 oz.

The doctor had to be called to give me some stitches. He had told me the day before when he had come to see Edward that he would see me at the surgery at two o'clock in the afternoon, so when he had to come out to visit me in the morning he laughed and said I had got the times mixed up.

Later that morning when the horrible nurse came in she said, 'I told you that you wouldn't have had the baby yet.'

'That's funny,' I replied. 'So what's that I've got in the nursery, then?'

It certainly put her in her place.

While I was at home being a full-time mother, my uncle Henry decided to move back to Colchester with his wife, Pat, and his son Henry.

My brother, Johnny, and I were pleased, as he would be nearer to us. He then got a job driving the corporation buses. Henry moved into the flat above me with his wife and young son, while she was expecting Keith. It was 1962 and I was pregnant at the time with Mary. Pat was also pregnant with their second child.

Pat was a little slow at picking things up and had no regard for hygiene as far as she or little Henry were concerned. I also tried to teach her how to cook as she was always burning things. One day, after the babies were born, Pat and I went to the antenatal clinic with Nanny Chaplin. Pat went in first to see the doctor and there was only a curtain to separate the doctor from other patients waiting to be seen. Nan and I felt ashamed when we heard the doctor tell Pat to make sure that before coming to the clinic in future she should have a bath. When we had finished in antenatal we went to get the babies weighed. I was flabbergasted when Pat undressed little Henry, as all Pat had put on him for a nappy was a dirty piece of rag. Neither had she brought a change of nappy for him. I had a couple spare so I gave her one of Edward's; no wonder little Henry had bad nappy rash.

When we left the clinic I asked Pat why little Henry had no nappies and she replied that they all needed washing. It wasn't mine or Nan's business to interfere in their lives, but her husband, Henry, went mad when he learned of the incident at the clinic that afternoon from Pat. He could be really nasty when he was angry and I could hear Henry shouting and throwing things. I felt sorry for Pat because he called her a 'dirty bitch', like my mother had done to me. When Henry had cooled down I heard the door slam as he went out. I waited for a while then went upstairs to see if Pat was all right. But she didn't seem to care; it was as if nothing was wrong.

Poor Pat wasn't very domesticated, either. It was smelly up in the flat and dirty nappies had been left in a bucket with no water to soak them. I helped Pat to clear up the room, took the dirty nappies down to my flat and put them in the bath with hot water, Dettol and some Napisan – a powder to help to keep the nappies white and help get the stains out. I left them to soak overnight then went back upstairs to tell Pat that if she had any washing to be done to bring it down in the morning so I could help her catch up. She didn't have a washing machine as the kitchen wasn't large enough, so it was no wonder Pat was getting behind with the washing; apparently, Henry did his own washing and ironing.

Henry didn't stop at the flat long. He bought a house near to where I was living but again wasn't happy. He asked my brother, Johnny, if he would like to swap houses and take over the mortgage. Henry would then live in the council house that Johnny was living in with his family. In the end he bought a caravan on a permanent caravan site. Not long after, Henry and Pat got divorced. Pat went back to Yarmouth with the two boys to live with her mother until she was allocated a council house. I didn't see a lot of Henry after he got divorced. He left the buses and started working for the army.

The next time I saw Henry was by chance, after I had married David. David and I were living at the flat in Dunwich Court, close to the army hospital. I was walking into town, when a car pulled up beside me. It was Henry and he gave me a lift into town. He told me that he hadn't been in touch because he knew that I was happily married and that I would be well looked after. He was living near the school that Rose went to when she came to live with David and me.

Sometime later I heard that Henry had moved away to live with a friend. Only my mother knew his new address but she wouldn't tell me. Years later he came to visit me at the flat when he was visiting Mother. I didn't recognise him at all and he had put on a lot of weight. He'd had a couple of heart attacks and had been diagnosed with diabetes. He could hardly walk or breathe very well, either, because of his asthma.

The next time I saw Henry was at Mother's funeral. Later, Henry decided to move back to his roots in Clacton. He moved house four more times before eventually settling down in Clacton, in rented accommodation, where a warden was on duty if he was taken ill at any time. Then one day Henry was taken into hospital, but he discharged himself, went home and passed away that night in his own bed in January 2012. He meant a lot to Johnny and me, especially in our childhood. He was also a spiritualist and I am sure he knew he was going die. Henry had told me earlier that he wanted to be in his own bed when the time came for him to die. I will miss him, because he was the only member in the family who kept in touch with me and my brother. He was always there for us if we needed anything and I shall remember him with great fondness.

When Mary was about fifteen months old I decided that I would return to work as my Aunt Pat said she would mind the children for me. I started back on the buses and so now Henry, Johnny and I were all working together. In fact, Henry and I used to change our shifts so that we could work together. We had some great times there. I remember one day when a passenger climbed on the bus and I had to ask them to wait for the next one as there was no room for her pushchair under the stairs, but she insisted on getting on anyway. I told her that the pushchair wasn't safe as we had open-end buses and it could easily roll off if it wasn't stowed under the stairway. After the fares were taken I would stand on the platform, from where I could keep an eye on things. Anyway, I was upstairs taking fares at the top of East Hill, when I looked out of the window and lo and behold, what did I see – the pushchair rolling down the hill!

The next stop was at the top of the high street – it used to be a one-way street then – where the passenger with the pushchair was getting off. When she asked me where her pushchair was, I explained that it must have been the one I had just seen rolling down East Hill. She swore at me, but I told her that it was her own fault as I had warned her that it wasn't safe where it was. Henry and I couldn't stop laughing about it when he heard what had happened.

I worked on the buses for about a year and then decided that I would become a full-time mother as I missed being with the children. Later that year I learnt that a church service was being held each week in the workmen's tin hut across the road from me on the land where St Charles Lucas School would be built later as the estate became bigger. I missed going to church, so I decided to try this one and took the children with me one Sunday. It was run by a Mr and Mrs Ibbertson and the pastor was John Bailey, whose wife, Jane, became a great friend of mine. They had three children: Jenny, Jeremy and Jeffrey.

The church was just starting up and they hoped one day to have their own building. When we had to leave the hut we held our services in John and Jane's home, which was also where Sunday school was held. Much later I became a Sunday school teacher to the little ones and I used to enjoy this immensely as I had always been a church person before I had got married. My son Jeremy used to go to the morning service with his great-grandmother and then to Sunday school in the afternoon. The church was eventually built on the Greenstead Estate.

At the time Jane was a childminder and she asked me if I would like to help out as she knew someone who needed one. She was unable to look after the children in question herself as she was only able to have a certain number of children under 5 years old, according to what you were registered for; it depended on the size of your accommodation. I said I would think it over and let her know.

I decided that I would accept her offer and got in touch with the authorities that dealt with applications. I enjoyed my work as a registered childminder and all the children I cared for were very dear to me. Apparently, they loved being with me and at the weekends when they were at home with their families, some of them cried because they wanted to go to Auntie Emily. It was probably because they missed playing with the other children. During the school holidays I also cared for their older siblings and when it came to dinner time I had to organise it in different sittings as there were so many of them; especially when Jane was on holiday as I used to look after the children that she minded as well. We were always good friends and helped each other whenever we could.

Light at the End of the Tunnel

Penny moved into the area at the same time as I did and we became good friends. If we weren't going out anywhere, we would be in each other's houses, usually in the mornings, nattering and drinking tea. Both of our husbands worked and it meant that the children could play and get to know each other, which was how I contracted the mumps. I remember the doctor telling me when he came out to see me on the evening of 23 February that you can catch the mumps if you have been in contact with the measles virus. The following morning I miscarried on my twenty-eighth birthday, in the middle of the night at home. I left a front door key with a note in an envelope for the doctor and when he arrived, he told me to stay in bed and that he would call the next morning as I had only been bleeding a little and there was still a chance the baby would survive. Neville had changed jobs and he now worked at the Eastern National bus station as a night cleaner. The doctor suggested that Neville should be contacted and that he should be at home looking after me and the children. Edward and Mary were at Jane and John's, which was a big help.

The doctor went to phone Neville's employer from a callbox three houses down and he spoke to the foreman on duty, explaining the situation. He then returned to wait for Neville to arrive home, to explain that he would have to take time off, which he was not best pleased about.

Jane came round just after the doctor had left. She came straight upstairs to see how I was feeling and she explained that the children had settled down for the night with her children. Edward was in with her two boys, Jeremy and Jeffrey, and Mary was in with her daughter,

Jenny. Jane told me she would look after them during the day time and would bring them home after they'd had their tea the following day. She knew Neville wasn't very good at looking after them, having never been left alone with the children before. I gave Jane a key so she could come and go as she pleased.

I miscarried a short while later. I knew I would have to call the doctor back, but left it until the morning, when Neville could go round to Jane's so that she could phone the doctor for me, as Neville didn't know how to use a phone. Neville was unable take in what had happened, so I told him to tell Jane that I had lost the baby. The doctor visited the home daily until I was well enough to get up, as I also had mumps.

I consider myself lucky to have good friends like Jane and John. There has been many a time when they have helped me out, when I was having trouble with Neville. He would disappear for days and weeks at a time, usually when there was a full moon, which appeared to affect him.

When I fell pregnant with Jeremy in late December 1967 we decided to ask the housing department if we could move to a larger house in Forest Road where new ones were being built and were eventually allocated one in the April. We moved in during the Easter week on 8 April and it was bitterly cold and snowing. I continued to do the child-minding as the older ones were now becoming teenagers and were able to help with the little ones.

One evening when I was doing a street collection for a children's charity, I met an old school friend of my brother's. His name was Tommy and he lived with his wife and three children. We all became good friends and helped each other out. The children often played together as they only lived a few doors away across the road.

Jeremy Edward was born on 23 September at two o'clock on a wet and stormy day. I could hear the thunder and the rain beating down on the window. Jane Bailey walked to school that afternoon to let Edward and Mary know that they had a baby brother and they were so excited that they ran back to tell their teachers.

Mary had started school at the beginning of that term, because if we had left it until Christmas she might have thought we were pushing her away because of the new baby. I found out while I was in the maternity home that Mary had been playing up at school because she couldn't have her own way and she had nearly put a chair through the glass door of the classroom. The headmistress even had to phone Jane on one occasion to ask how she handled her when she was in this mood. Jane told her that the best way was to ignore her completely. Her poor behaviour continued right through her infant years and every day she ended up in the headmistress' office, where they took off her shoes so that she was unable to hurt herself or anyone else with her kicking and screaming until she calmed down. Mary was a stubborn child and became even more of a problem in later years.

Seven Year Itch/Married Bliss?

In 1970 I started to have problems with Neville. He used to go off on a Friday after he had been paid and not come back home until days after, leaving me and the children without any money and with nothing to eat. This was when I found out who all my friends were. They looked after us time and again, but it was embarrassing for me and I knew I had to do something about it. He was also demanding to have sex all the time, which was getting me down as I hated every minute of it, especially after what had happened to me in my early years. I know that was a bit unfair, but I didn't know what to do.

Things got so bad that eventually I wrote a letter to the doctor. Knowing that Neville was unable to read, I asked him to take it to the surgery for me, telling him that it was for a prescription. The doctor knew that I was having trouble with him, as I was already on antidepressants, and I don't know what he said to him, but he didn't bother me for sex after that for some time.

The problem got worse over the next two years and it didn't help much that my brother and his family had moved in to a house at the back of us and could see all of what was going on. It wasn't my brother who was stirring up trouble but his wife. She wore the trousers in that house and was telling my parents everything that was going on. I never liked her from the first time I met her and later that year we decided to do a house exchange with a family in Spruce Avenue, to get away from my brother's wife.

We were not far from where Jane and John were living, so I was able to go round if I was feeling a bit down. In fact, I was round there most mornings as I had given up childminding since all the children were now old enough to look after themselves until their parents got home. Sometimes I went round to Jane's to mind the children that she looked after so that she could go to take photographs of people's children. It was her new hobby and she was very good at it.

Things weren't getting any better and my nerves were getting worse. My doctor wasn't very happy with the state I was in and he was concerned. He told me that if something wasn't done soon, he would have to intervene as it was affecting the children.

One weekend when Neville had gone off on one of his disappearing acts, I decided that I'd had enough. The rent wasn't getting paid and we hadn't much to eat in the house. I made up my mind to file for a divorce on the grounds of mental cruelty, backed up by my doctor. When Neville finally came home I told him what I was going to do, but it went in one ear and out of the other.

The next few weeks went on as normal until one morning he came into the bedroom with a cup of coffee in one hand and a five-pound note in the other. He then had the nerve to ask if he could have sex for £5. I was so furious and upset that I tipped the coffee over him and told him to get out. Later that morning I went to see my doctor to tell him what had happened. He couldn't stop laughing as it was the funniest thing he had heard for ages. After he had calmed down he apologised for laughing, saying that the way I had said it had sounded really funny. He then asked me what I was going to do about it and that's when I told him that I was going to start divorce proceedings, which I did.

Neville didn't come home that evening and the next day I made an appointment to see a solicitor. I also went to see social security to explain my situation and they were able to give me a giro payment that day so that I could at least feed the children.

Later that week when Neville returned I told him that he couldn't come in until he had put his dirty boots in the shed. While he was doing so, I bolted all the doors to the house to keep him out. Then I told him that I was filing for a divorce and he was to find somewhere else to live. I explained that I was now claiming Income Support but that he was still responsible for the rent unless he signed the tenancy over to me. That week he slept in the shed and continued to go to work as normal. Neville was working as a dustman at the time and when the dustmen came round, as his team did our area I asked the driver to give Neville his belongings, which I had placed in a suitcase. The driver took them and left them at the office for Neville to collect when he returned from his round. I knew most of the dustmen as they worked with Neville and I used to give them a drink whenever they reached my house. Neville never came back to the house and I managed to get him to sign a letter I had written handing over the tenancy of the house to me.

While I was married to Neville, he introduced me to one of his workmates. His name was David and it was love at first sight. At the time I knew that I had to put him out of my mind, not only because I was married, but also because David had a partner and two young daughters of his own, as well as providing for his partner's other three children. There was no way that I would break up a family – I had learnt that lesson in my earlier years when I was in Scotland.

I got on well with David's partner and used to visit her sometimes in the afternoon. The two youngest girls were David's. Susan was the oldest at 2 years old and June was just a year old. They had beautiful auburn hair and blue eyes, just like their dad's. I remained friendly with their mother for some time, even after David had split up with her.

David moved into a room above Cackets, the barbers, which he shared with my ex-husband. I don't know how it came about, but somehow I got a letter to him to say he could come and visit me if he wanted to. I was still seeing his ex-wife and had asked her if she had split for good, which she told me that she had.

It was late summer when he eventually called round and he was a bit down in the dumps as his ex was giving him a hard time and had stopped him from seeing his girls, whom he lived for. She had always had Social Services involvement even before she had met David and the children were often put into foster care so she could have some respite.

As time went on David went backwards and forwards to his ex, but only when it suited her. David and I still saw each other at times, but just for a chat and a bit of company. I loved him but never said anything as his children meant the world to him and I was just happy to be able to share him.

Jeremy started school after Christmas in 1974. He got on well at school and was liked by all the teachers. They couldn't believe that he was Mary's brother as he was so well behaved in comparison and would share anything that he could with his classmates. On his sixth birthday he wanted a birthday party, so I asked him whom he wanted to invite.

He wanted the entire class to come, so I ended up with twenty children. It was a lovely sunny September day and I put the tables and chairs in the back garden where they had plenty of room to run around so I had no mess in the house.

Once Jeremy had started school, I decided it would be nice to get a part-time job as I missed not having him around. The estate on which I lived was growing larger and we now had a few shops in the square. A new fish and chip shop had just opened and was advertising for part-time staff, so I plucked up courage and went in. I was offered the job and started the next day, working lunchtimes and on Wednesday and Friday evenings. Edward was old enough to look after Jeremy in the evenings and if not, I had a good boss and his wife would let me take him into work with me. He used to stay with her above the shop while I was working. My boss' name was Graham and they had a little boy called Mathew, who Jeremy used to play with.

In the summer that year I remember going to Walton Beach with David and his two girls. It was one of the rare times that his ex let him have the children for the day. I only had Jeremy to take as Edward and Mary were doing other things now they were older and felt they were too big to be going out with Mum. That was the last summer he went to the seaside, but he enjoyed the day with Susan and June, even though they couldn't go on the beach as the tide was in. We took them to the pier instead, where they enjoyed the rest of the day on the rides and they all went home tired and happy children.

That year we were all taken to Coventry by Miss Richardson to see the cathedral and to buy Jeremy his first Bible, which was white, and another for me. Miss Richardson, whom I now call my mum, was the children's godmother. She bought it for him as he went to church and Sunday school every week with his great-grandmother and she was determined that he should have one before he got christened. Nan used to come over to our house every Sunday and during the holidays.

On the day we went to Coventry Miss Richardson asked me if I would consider having Jeremy christened properly as the other two children had already been christened; Edward at St Johns in Great Clacton and Mary at St Andrews on the Greenstead Estate. As Jeremy had only had a naming ceremony at the church I went to, I agreed that she could arrange it as she wanted it to be held at St John's Church where she knew the vicar well. It was organised for early September 1974, just before Jeremy's seventh birthday, and Miss Richardson was to be his godmother. The weather was still warm and the christening party was to be held at Miss Richardson's home in the garden afterwards.

The week before the christening Jeremy was so excited that he told his teacher at school, but at the time his teacher thought he had made a mistake and told him that only babies got christened. The day after his christening he asked if he could take a piece of his cake for his teacher and also his presents that he had been given so he could show her. I took him to school that morning so I could bring them all back and when his teacher heard all about it, she told me what she had said, thinking he had got mixed up with something else. I explained to her that the Sunday school where he went only did a naming ceremony as a baby, and his teacher apologised, saying that he had been right all the time.

Signpost of Sorrow

Just before his seventh birthday, Jeremy asked if he would be able to have a party like he'd had the previous year and to invite all of his class friends again. I was a bit reluctant about it at first but I'm glad that I did because as it turned out it was the last one that he was to have.

The week before his birthday he kept asking his teacher if he would see a signpost when he went to heaven. The teacher put this down to the fact that he went to church and Sunday school and thought no more of it. That week he also drew a map with a signpost pointing to heaven, as well as two grave stones. One signpost said 'you live' and the other said 'you die'.

The weekend before his birthday I took him to town to buy some new clothes. His favourite colour was red and he picked out a red shirt with a navy trim, navy trousers, red vest, pants and red socks. He told me he wanted these for somewhere special. I naturally thought they were for Sunday as it was harvest festival the next day. That was the last Sunday he went to church with his great-nan.

The following Wednesday on 1 October was the big fight for Muhammad Ali, which was being shown that night on the TV. David had asked if he could come round to watch it, which he did. That evening Jeremy was late coming in for his evening meal as he had gone to play at a friend's house. He came in about half an hour before I had to leave for work. I had time to give him his meal and then I asked him if he wanted to come to work with me or stay with Jane as Edward had gone to a football match and Mary had gone to band practice. He said that he wanted to stay with David and that if he drilled a hole in David's head, David would remember to build the model plane that he had been given for his birthday. What he didn't know was that David had already done the model and it was on top of the wardrobe drying. I was quite happy to let him stay as Jeremy loved David, who was always playing with him and the other children whenever he came to visit. Before I left, David asked if it would be all right to have a bath as he had come straight from work on the dustcarts and I said that it would be fine.

I went to work as normal and on Wednesday nights we always had a big order for chips for the bingo club at the hall up the road. I used to start getting the order ready at 7.30 p.m. and they used to pick it up themselves. I was in the middle of doing this, when David came rushing in and told me that I had to come right away as Jeremy had had an accident and that the ambulance was waiting for me. He was pretty upset and was unable to tell me what had happened. I reached where we cut through to get to the house, when I saw the ambulance driver. For some reason or other, I knew that Jeremy was dead.

We were taken to the hospital, but Jeremy was pronounced dead on arrival. I was too shocked even to be able to cry or to say anything. David and I had just been given a cup of tea, when the police arrived and took us to the station – David in one car and me in the other. I don't know which was worse – the loss of Jeremy or being treated like a criminal. David was taken upstairs to be questioned and I was downstairs. They asked where Jeremy usually got undressed when he had a bath, how long had I known David and loads of other questions. The police kept coming down to see if my answers were consistent with what David was telling them and the interrogation seemed endless. It was 3.30 a.m. before they took us home and they already had the forensic team at the house.

Edward and Mary were over at Janice and Douglas' house, one of our neighbours. Douglas had been helping David to try to revive Jeremy. As it was late they had put them to bed and they stayed there until morning. David and I never went to bed that night as we were too upset to do anything. It was then that David told me what had happened. Apparently, Jeremy had asked if he could have a bath as well, which he did. He also asked David if he could play in the bath with his toys, as I usually let him do this after he had washed. David said that he could and went to turn the fire on in the front room so it was warm for when they watched the big fight.

David said he kept calling upstairs to see if he was all right and when he didn't answer, he assumed he was hiding and playing a game. Eventually he went upstairs and I can only imagine what it felt like when he found him under the water, especially as he was looking after him. It could easily have been when he was with me, as I always let him play in the bath. Sometimes I would forget he was there and he would get out by himself and come downstairs.

I tried to phone the children's godmother, my 'mum', but was unable to get hold of her as she was away at the time. So I rang my parents instead. I can't remember who answered the phone, but I heard my sister shout to them that something had happened to Jeremy. I told them that he had had an accident and had died, and they said they would come to Colchester later that day.

I went round to Mary and Graham's at the fish shop early that morning to let them know what had happened. They were both very upset and told me to take as much time as I needed and that if I needed any help they would be there for me. They said I wasn't to worry about the funeral expenses and that they would settle it and make arrangements for me to pay them back each week out of my wages.

The hardest thing for me was to tell Edward and Mary when they came home the next morning. I didn't send them to school that day and phoned Jane to ask her to contact the school for me and to let them know what had happened.

When the children returned home on the morning following Jeremy's death, Edward had already guessed that Jeremy was no longer with us. A short while later, Edward disappeared at ten o'clock one morning and I found out later that he had gone to his school, where he was stopped by one of the teachers because he wasn't wearing school uniform. He explained that he wasn't in uniform because he wasn't coming into school because his little brother had just died. The following Friday his teacher came round to see me and asked if he could take Edward back to him and his wife's home for a few days to give him a break, to which I agreed. Mary sobbed her heart out when she learned of Jeremy's death and it was following his death that she started all her problems, playing truant, not concentrating in class and generally getting into trouble.

My parents didn't like David much, but only because they didn't know him and because my brother's wife had been stirring it, so David said he would make himself scarce while my parents came to see me. By the time they arrived they had already been round to my brother's house above the Co-op opposite the fish shop where I worked, to see if they knew what had happened, but they didn't because I hadn't told them. Instead, they heard it from my parents. They all came round in force, shouting that David was to blame and telling me that it was my fault as I hardly knew him and shouldn't have left Jeremy with him. I told them that for their information we had known David for four years and that if that was all they could say by way of support I would be better off without them.

Mary asked if she could go back to stay with my parents, so I let her as she was upset enough as it was and didn't need me creating difficulties for her. Just as they were leaving there was a knock at the front door. It was a lady who I assumed was a policewoman as the police had told me that someone would be coming round to see me and so I thought nothing of it at the time. But it turned out that it wasn't the police and just before I shut the door having let her in, a police car pulled up outside and the policewoman asked me if I knew who the lady was. I replied that I didn't and later discovered that she was from the *Evening Gazette.* She asked me if it was possible to have a photograph of Jeremy and the policewoman said that I didn't have to talk to her, but I said that it was all right. I gave her a photo which had just been taken at school and told her that I wanted it back.

After the reporter had gone, the policewoman said that she needed to escort me to the morgue to identify Jeremy's body as they were going to do a post-mortem later that day. It was one of the worst things I have ever had to do, especially as a mother; after all, you are supposed to die before your children.

The following day the police came to tell me that the results of the post-mortem had come back OK and that there was no foul play indicated, which I already knew as I was certain that David would never harm a child. The only thing he blamed himself for was that he was unable to save Jeremy. When you know someone who has lost someone owing to tragic circumstances, especially someone so young who had their whole lives ahead of them, it's the little things that become important and you learn to value what you've got and to treasure each moment.

I was still waiting for the inquest when I heard that my father was determined that he was going to go. He was still insisting that David, who was minding Jeremy at the time of the accident and whom I married later in 1986, had done some harm to Jeremy. I was furious. David and I had been questioned at the police station on the evening of the accident and they were satisfied with the statements that had been given, so why couldn't my father leave things alone? They asked where Jeremy usually undressed and if I let him stay in the bath on his own to play.

I decided not to tell Edward I'd had a telephone call from the police advising me that the inquest date had finally been arranged for 14 November, which was on a Friday, at Colchester Court in the afternoon. At least if he didn't know then my father couldn't pressurise him. I had been asked to contact the witnesses, David and Douglas. Douglas lived across the road from us and he had tried to help David revive Jeremy. Mary stayed with John and Jane Bailey whenever I was working as I couldn't leave her and Edward on their own as they would argue.

It was then that I learnt who my true friends were. Most people did nothing as they didn't know how to respond to such tragic information, so I wasn't exactly inundated with visitors. I felt very alone. Mary was staying with my parents and Edward with his teacher. At the time, I had no feeling whatsoever. I didn't cry, either. I didn't even cry at the funeral. It was only later when I was taken into hospital after an overdose that it really hit and I broke down and sobbed, having tried to take my own life. It was then that my life fell apart.

When David's children came home from foster care he moved back in with his ex and the children. I understood why – it was only natural that he would want to be with his two girls. But it meant that I was on my own again at a time when I really needed his support.

News soon got around as it was in the newspaper and as I was well known at the fish shop, customers were asking where I was. One of my customers worked for the Co-op Funeral Parlour and asked his employer if he could personally visit me to arrange Jeremy's funeral. Because there was going to be an inquest I was unsure whether the funeral could even go ahead, but the man told me that the police had released Jeremy's body.

At the inquest, there was just Douglas, David and myself who were questioned. All I can assume is that Jeremy must have lay underneath the water, like he did in the swimming pool, which I'd told him not to do. That is the only way I can think that it must have happened. If I'd been at home myself, he wouldn't have had a bath because he suffered with congestive lungs. The verdict was that his lungs were three quarters full of mucus and one quarter of water – he'd just died instantly. The coroner said that nothing could have been done to save him. We are always talking about him and to this day, David still blames himself and he frequently says he should have been able to save him.

The pastor, John Bailey, asked if I would mind if he didn't take Jeremy's funeral service as it would be like burying one of his own children, so Jeremy's godmother made an appointment to see the vicar who had christened Jeremy, to ask if he would be able to take the service instead. Whilst he didn't take the service, John did hold a dedication service for Jeremy so all of the congregation and the children who went to Sunday school could celebrate his life by singing his favourite hymns, including 'The Lord of the Dance'.

We arranged the funeral for Tuesday, 14 October 1975 at 11.00 a.m. I asked if I would be able to see Jeremy at the chapel of rest, so he gave me his personal phone number and said that he would take me himself on Sunday if Jeremy was fit to see depending on what they had done during the post-mortem. He told me to phone up first to see if it was advisable, which I did, but I was told that he wouldn't be ready until the Monday.

The day before the funeral I organised for him to be dressed in the clothes that he had picked for his birthday. I often wondered if that was why he had picked them, as I have been told that when it is your time to go you know. I gave him his favourite toys, his Bible and a little cross to take with him. He looked so lovely and it was as if he was just sleeping. I asked the rest of the family to go outside so that I could have a little time with him by myself. I said my goodbyes in peace then kissed him gently for the last time. My son, Jeremy – too special for this world, as the saying goes.

The following morning, on the day of the funeral, I was angry to discover that my family had gone against my express wishes and had bought wreaths instead of cut flowers. As I had opted for a cremation, I wanted take the flowers to the residential home on the estate for the elderly folk to enjoy rather than have them going to waste in a bin.

There were masses of people in attendance at Jeremy's funeral and all his classmates had taken little bunches of flowers to school that morning for his teacher to bring with her. It was touching that so many people cared so much for him. After the funeral we all went back to my house. My parents stayed for about fifteen minutes before leaving to go round to my brother's – that's how much they cared about me. They took Mary with them, which I wasn't too pleased about as my father was on annual leave at home and my mother was at work at the time. But at least my sister, Sandra, was still at home during the daytime and I knew that she would keep an eye on her. Sandra was studying at college in the evenings, by which time my mother would be home from work, so at least I didn't need to worry about her safety.

On Friday nights after I had left for work, my father kept ringing Edward to ask when the inquest was being held as he was determined to find out what had happened that night, even though I had told him that it was an accident and that the police had confirmed it the day after the post-mortem.

The only members of family I had contact with after Jeremy's funeral were my sister, Sandra, and my uncle Henry; the rest of the family didn't want to know me. I was so glad that it was all over and that I could start to come to terms with my loss and what had happened. At least now I could try to get on with my life for the sake of Edward and Mary.

Old Haunts

The following summer in August 1976 Edward and Mary were going away with the Sunday school club, which was held on Friday evenings, to a church camp. They were supposed to be away for one week and on their return, Edward was going camping for a week with the army cadets, which he had joined two years earlier. Mary was also going to be away the same week in Belgium with the school.

As they were both away for two weeks it meant that I would be on my own at home. Graham had closed the shop for the same two weeks for our summer holiday, so it wasn't long before my father got in touch with me to see if bridges could be mended. I agreed I would patch things up with him and I was glad in a way. They still didn't like David, but I had lost contact with him anyway when he moved back to live with his family and went to work in a different town, so it wasn't going to be an issue.

I asked my father if he would ring my Uncle Reuben, his younger brother, to see if I could visit him and Aunt Gladys, his wife, while Edward and Mary were away. Uncle Reuben gave my father his number and when I phoned, he was glad I had rung and said I would be welcome to stay with them any time I wanted.

The following day I went into town to make the arrangements for my two-week stay and that evening I rang Uncle Reuben and gave the details for my arrival in Birmingham. I only intended to stay for the first week as I needed to get back to see Edward and Mary before they went off on their second holiday. They would also want clean clothing and Edward would need his cadet uniform and camping gear. He had saved up all his pocket money and any money he had earned from doing little jobs locally.

Jane, a good friend of mine, and her husband had told me I needed a break after the last ten months, what with all we had been through, and they agreed to sort Edward and Mary out for me so I could go for the full two weeks. I spoke to both children and they were quite happy with the arrangement as they had stayed with Jane and John when I had trouble with Neville before I divorced him.

Some of the children from Sunday school had to leave camp a day earlier as they were going on holiday with their own families. The local factories closed down for two weeks every year and it just so happened that it was the same two weeks. This was the only time the factory workers could take their holidays, so the church group left a day early on the Friday so the children would be back in time. Edward was due to leave on the Sunday morning and Mary was scheduled to leave on the Monday. I left all the children's gear with Jane and also a key in case I had forgotten anything.

Once Edward and Mary had left I started to sort out my own clothing for my stay with Uncle Reuben. I didn't need much as my aunt had a washing machine which I could use. I also took Jeremy's photo albums as Aunt Gladys and Uncle Reuben had never seen the children. All I had to do was to leave the house tidy and have a bath the following morning so I would be fresh and comfortable for the seven-hour journey.

When I arrived in Birmingham I was greeted with a big hug from Uncle Reuben and then we caught the bus to my his house. Uncle Reuben lived in the same area where I had lived with Little Nan during the war. I was looking forward to seeing my cousins and venturing into the city to see how things had changed.

On the first morning we went into the city centre. I still recognised most of it and we must have walked for miles.

When we arrived back home we had a long rest and a welcome cup of tea made by myself. It had been a long day for us all and thankfully none of us needed an evening meal as we had eaten out.

The rest of the week was spent visiting all my cousins, who were all married with children of their own. I took lots of photographs to take back home to remind me of the lovely time I'd had and I also visited my aunt's family, who remembered me from when I was younger. The first week went in a flash and we spent the second week visiting all my favourite haunts where I had spent my happiest year in 1942. I started with the school, which still looked the same. Then I made my way to the old fever hospital and in its place was a brand-new hospital. I walked along the road where I had lived during the war until I could see the playing field, passing all the shops which also still looked the same.

When I reached Nan's old house, standing at the front gate was Mr Beasley, my best friend Janet's dad, who remembered me well. We spoke about Janet and of the time when I had lived next door with Nan. Apparently, I had just missed his wife. I asked for Janet's address so I could get back in touch with her and when I knocked on her door Janet couldn't believe her eyes. She said I hadn't changed a bit, just older. We talked about old times and about our lives leading up to now. Janet asked if I would like to join her and her friends that night at bingo. I was thrilled to bits as I had never been to a bingo hall. It was at the ABC picture house and the last time I had been there was when I was living with my nan. The evening would be a lovely way to finish off my holiday as I was going home the next day.

While I was staying with my aunt and uncle, one morning I retrieved the mail from the floor and noticed the surname on the front of the envelope had been spelt wrongly. I pointed this out when I handed him the mail and he told me that the spelling was correct, so I asked if he knew why my surname was spelt without the letter 'i' in Grainger. My uncle explained that when my father joined the army, there were two David Graingers in same regiment but in different sections and as neither of them had a middle name, they were asked if one of them would change their surname so things didn't get mixed up. My father agreed because the other David was always in trouble and spent a lot of time in the detention centre. Apparently, my father was sent to the detention centre by mistake once and wasn't prepared to let it happen again.

Life Goes On, or Does It?

It was hard for me and the children that year at Christmas and none of us could get into the Christmas spirit. Even my gran, who always came round to our house during the holidays, found it hard – it was so empty not having Jeremy there with us, and also David.

David spent Christmas with his children and I found myself feeling very down without both him and Jeremy. I had left the other two children with my gran and went out for a walk. I must have wandered around St John's Estate for hours and it was dark when I eventually sat down on a bench. I can't even remember what I was thinking. I felt dead inside. Being the first Christmas and not having Jeremy there broke my heart. I didn't even think about the two children that I did have at the time, I was so low.

All of a sudden, the children's godmother pulled up in the car with a friend. I can only assume that Edward had rung her as I hadn't returned home and she'd come out looking for me. Miss Richardson and her friend took me back to where David was staying with his partner and daughters. Miss Richardson knocked on the door and brought him out to me. We chatted and I said that I understood why he had gone back to his partner and we parted tearfully.

Miss Richardson said she would take me back to her bungalow to stay with her and she called out her doctor, who gave me a sedative of some sort which put me out for the rest of the night. Not that I knew any difference, as I was more or less out of it anyway. The children stayed with John and Jane Bailey and I stayed with Miss Richardson for a couple of weeks before I was well enough to go home.

Following his death, every October thereafter I became depressed and the following year I ended up back in Severalls. In Severalls, I became unruly for whatever reason, and they were forced to put me in a padded cell so I couldn't do any harm to myself or others. I knew I'd been taken there and I'd been taken against my wishes. I remember kicking and screaming to get out of the door and I was given a sedative. Since then, I have never liked doors to be shut or locked and I still don't even now.

The following day, Miss Richardson came to see me and I was let out of the padded cell but I had to stay in a locked ward for three to four weeks, at which point I was taken to a rehabilitation centre called Mile End Court, in the same grounds. During this period, the only visitors I received were Miss Richardson and my Uncle Henry. By the time I was moved into the rehabilitation centre I felt better as I was on some medication and I was also under a counsellor. I hadn't been offered any counselling when Jeremy died as no one had ever thought about it.Had I done so at the time, I may not have become as low as I did. Although every October was the same. It has taken twenty years for me to reach the stage where I no longer find myself slipping into a low mood in October.

I realise now that it was Bernard Balls and Maureen Flynn, mediums from the church, who got me through it. I was a Christian at the time and I believed in the afterlife, but it was them who told me that he was all right. Jeremy hadn't died, only his body – his soul was in Heaven and he was looking down on me. When I worked in the fish and chip shop, a Jehovah's Witness came to my door the day that Jeremy had died and she told me that Jeremy hadn't gone up to Heaven, because there were no spaces up there for him. At the time I told her to go away and never come to my doorstep again. After that, I never served her in the chip shop again. But knowing what these two spiritualists from the church had told me made me feel better and it was through them that I began my recovery process.

After Christmas when I went back to work, Graham told me that he was giving up the shop but that my job would be secure with the new owners. I got on well with the new owners and when Edward turned fourteen they gave him a Saturday job and he also worked during the school holidays, which turned full time when he left school.

In 1977 my father was taken into hospital. My sister phoned me when I was at work to let me know that he was in Essex County Hospital and that he was very ill. I told Edward about my father but not Mary as she idolised her grandfather and if he was as bad as my sister had led me to believe, she would be very upset, so I decided not to tell her until I had been to the hospital myself to see how bad he really was.

I didn't want to go to see him but my sister told me that I should as all the family were down from Birmingham. Apparently, my mother didn't want me to know about my father's illness. She had never treated me like a daughter but more like an outcast all my life. I know this must sound awful, but I decided to go just to see if he really was on his way out, as in some way I felt it would make me feel better after what he had done and perhaps allow me to move on.

It was the day after my birthday on 25 February 1977, which was a Saturday, that Edward and I went to the hospital in the evening. All the family were there. I don't know what had been said, but apart from my sister I was completely ignored. If only they had known the truth about my father – I wonder if they would have acted any different ... Before we left the hospital the doctor called my mother into the office to tell her that they didn't think that he would last until the morning.

On Sunday morning I got a phone call from my sister to say that he had passed away in the early hours of the morning. In a way I was glad. I hated my father for what he had done, taking my childhood away from me. Memories are etched in my brain that I will never be able to blot out. It wasn't just sexual abuse; it was rape, where he forced me to have sex after I had got married. I am sorry to say that I was happy that he had gone and with him, 'our little secret'.

I didn't know how I was going to tell Mary. I was at John and Jane Bailey's at the time and Sandra had rung them as we weren't on the phone. I told John what had happened and he said he would tell Mary when they got back from church as Mary would be with them. John and Jane were good with her and I think Mary looked upon John as a father figure.

By this time my brother had moved to Clacton, to live near our parents. He and my mother didn't always get on, especially if he was in contact with me. Now that he was living further away from me, we didn't have as much contact as we used to. Mother always blamed me for ruining her life. She had never wanted to get married, but in the 1960s couples who were having a baby were forced to marry or they would bring shame on the family. Those who didn't marry were sent to an institution and often never came out again. A friend of my mother was put in an institution and my friend was put in care as a result. When I was old enough I told my mother it wasn't my fault that she got pregnant and that she should have taken precautions if she disliked me that much.

My brother took care of all the arrangements for the funeral and at that time he and my mother were getting on well together. My sister phoned to say that I would be picked up on the Friday at 7.30 a.m. from my mother's home and that we would be taken to the funeral from there. I decided that I would like to go to see my father at the chapel of rest, but it was in Clacton and I realised that if I went on the bus I wouldn't be able to get there and back in time to start work at 4.30 p.m. I knew that my sister-in-law would be at her mother's house and so I phoned to see if she would take me to Clacton when I finished work on the Wednesday, but she said that she wasn't going to see her mother that day and so I left it at that.

On the Wednesday lunchtime when I left work I was very angry to see my sister-in-law's car outside her mother's. She must have forgotten that I passed her mum's house every time I went to work when she chose to lie to me that day.

When I got home I went round to Jane's to see if I could make a phone call to my mother's. My sister answered and I told her how I felt about my sister-in-law. Her answer was that no one wanted to take me to the funeral either, so I told her that I wouldn't be going to the funeral and that if I did change my mind I would make my own way there. My sister wasn't very happy about my decision and said she couldn't tell them that, so I gave her an excuse and told her to tell them I wasn't going as it was too near to Jeremy's funeral and so too painful for me.

On the Friday things were getting the better of me, so I went to see my doctor earlier that morning to have a talk to him and explain what was going on. He told me that I should go to the funeral as I would regret it later, but I knew that I wouldn't owing to what my father had done to me; it was too late to go anyway by this time as the service was about to begin. He gave me a prescription and said he wanted me to make an appointment for the following week to see how I was. I felt better for seeing him and went home to get ready for work.

I went to work as usual and was fine until the lunchtime rush, when my Uncle Henry came into the shop. He was on our bus route and had called in to see why I hadn't gone to the funeral and why I hadn't sent any flowers. I was angry but was too busy to speak to him. He couldn't stop anyway as his bus was due out, so he said he would see me in the evening when I finished work as on Friday nights I finished early.

That evening when he came round I explained what had been going on and he was angry as he had told the family from the beginning that he would take me with him to the funeral, but they had told him firmly that I had to leave from the family home. I asked him what he meant when he said there were no flowers from us and he said there was a display from the children but was told that there was nothing from me. I told him that I had sent flowers and that if they weren't there I would go down to the florists to see why not as I had paid for them; I even showed him the receipt. Instead of things getting better, things were getting worse. Thanks to my mother and my brother I had lost what family I had apart from my gran and my uncle Henry.

After Mary and Graham sold the shop it wasn't the same and I decided to leave, which wasn't the best thing to have done as it gave me too much time to dwell on things. I was becoming increasingly depressed and even suicidal, not wanting to get up in the mornings or do anything. I still hadn't come to terms with losing Jeremy and I hadn't been able to cry, instead bottling it all up inside.

One morning it reached the stage where I could take no more and after the children had gone to school I decided to take my own life. I took all the tablets I had in the house and stayed in bed. I don't know much after that except that I awoke in hospital. I learnt afterwards that Edward had called in to see Jane to tell her that I was staying in bed and that he was worried. It was Jane who had found me and sent for an ambulance.

Later that day I was sent to Severalls Hospital to get treatment. As always it was my Uncle Henry who was first to visit me, bringing things that I would need while I was there. The following day my 'darling' mother came with my brother and his wife. All I got from them was a telling off to the effect that I might have thought about Mother as it was only a couple of months since Father had died. Anger made its way to the surface and I told them I didn't need them and that they had only come to gloat and to appease their own consciences. I also told them that it was partly their fault that I was in this state before asking them to leave and telling them not to come back.

Later that day I was transferred to Myland Court, which was where people were sent when they were suffering from a mental illness. I was there for some time and Mary went to stay with Maureen Flynn, whom I knew from the spiritualist church which I used to go to. Bernard Balls, the former president of the church, and Maureen came to see me at the hospital and told me they had been looking for me since Jeremy's accident but that they were unable to find out where I had moved, as I was now living in Larch Close near to Jane and John. John wasn't very happy at the time as I had also changed my religion when I was told I could no longer teach Sunday school because of my divorce. They came to tell me that one of Maureen's daughters was getting married and I was allowed out to go to the wedding with Mary. Mary got on well with the family and they became friends.

When Bernard decided stand down from being president, he offered the church and the job of president to Irene Foley and he took over playing the church organ. Irene is a very friendly person who welcomed all people who entered the church. After the service the congregation are invited to stay and have tea and coffee with biscuits. Sometimes there would be cake, which Gloria, one of the committee members, would bake; it gave the congregation a chance to catch up with one another.

There were four ladies on the committee and three gentlemen. The ladies were Irene, the president, Gloria, vice-president, June, who was responsible for arranging the medium speakers, and Jenny, who was the secretary. The three gentlemen were Ray, Peter and Sean. All of these people have played a big part in my life, helping me and explaining the spiritual way of life. They also helped me to come to terms with any problems from my past, large or small, and I have had my share of them over the years. I will always look on the church as my second home and family. If it had not been for the church, I would probably have not been here to tell my story.

After a few bouts in hospital I gradually came to terms with what had happened and started to get my life back on track. I had lost contact with David as he had moved away to work but I still had contact with his ex and his children. Later, I moved to Barnhall Estate with Mary, as Edward had moved out because we weren't getting on. He had a full-time job and so could support himself.

One night I got a phone call from Graham, my previous employer. He was now working at his father-in-law's fish shop and restaurant and one of his staff had let him down. He was ringing to see if I could go in to help him out. It was a cold and snowy night, so I had to walk into town as the buses weren't running to time. It was as if I had never been away and I enjoyed being back so he offered me a job, which I was glad to accept as it would give me something to do.

Mary was now in her teenage years and getting hard to handle. She often played truant from school and we argued a lot. Eventually, a social worker came to see me as she was getting out of control. Customers were coming into the shop and telling Graham that they had seen her in different pubs, hanging out with soldiers. As we weren't able to see eye to eye, the social worker put her into foster care, at Mary's request.

We had always argued since she was a teenager and she didn't like living with me as she said I didn't give her enough space or let her stop out late. She asked me to get a social worker so she could go into care as she didn't want to live with me any more. I was upset, but at least I felt calmer and didn't have to keep worrying about her whereabouts. This meant I could concentrate on my work instead of listening to people coming into the fish shop telling me what she was up to.

I only saw one social worker and she asked what I wanted. I said that it wasn't up to me and that if Mary wanted to go into care then let her. She would probably find out whether it was better to stay at home or go into foster care if this was the case and at least get it out of her system. She went that day and that night I felt empty. I also felt a sense of relief, as I was so fed up with arguing with her. I obviously hoped she'd come back but didn't know if it would be any different, as she was a wayward teenager, going into her thirteenth year when she was taken into care. I guess I was past caring. Edward was already living elsewhere, Jeremy had died and now Mary and I weren't getting on. I just needed some peace in my life and to get my life back on track.

After a few weeks she was asking to come home, but it wasn't long before she was up to her old tricks of skipping school again. She used to get on the bus to go to school but didn't arrive there. I felt powerless to do anything about it. I felt that only the social workers or somebody else could sort her out. Then one day she didn't return home and after ringing around a few people she knew I had to report her missing. I was worried for her safety, not knowing her whereabouts.

A few weeks later I had a phone call at work by the police to tell me that she had been found and that she was now in a children's home, just outside Chelmsford. It was a Saturday and Graham and Mary said they would take me to see her on the Sunday. After Mary had got into trouble and had been taken into care, Edward came to see me to mend bridges. He has always worried about me and always tried to make things better for me. Edward came with me to see Mary, as we were now back on speaking terms.

When we arrived, Graham said that they would drive round for a while and collect us in an hour. One of the workers at the home took us to where Mary was, but judging by the reception we got from her we could have saved Graham the journey. I had taken her some new trainers as requested and they were thrown back at me. All I got was a mouthful of abuse. I told the worker that I wouldn't be visiting her again until she requested my presence and could talk civilly, without all the foul language.

Mary was given a twenty-eight-day order and was to appear in court, which I had to attend. When I arrived I learnt from the police officer who was giving evidence that she had been found naked under a man's bed. It turned out to be someone I knew not far from where I lived. When Mary was on the stand the judge asked her if I was able to control her, to which she replied no, with the result that another twenty-eight-day order was placed on her and she was required to appear in court again.

During the time she was waiting to go back to court she disappeared and no one knew where she had gone. When the date for her court appearance came round she still hadn't been found and a warrant was put out for her arrest. Meanwhile, Mary had decided to go to social services, where she was arrested and taken to court. The judge then gave an order for her to be taken into care until she was eighteen.

I continued working at the fish shop and got to know a customer quite well as he used to come into the restaurant most nights to have his tea. One evening he asked me if I would go out with him. He was a lot older than me but I was so fed up being by myself that I thought it would be company for us both and that was all I wanted.

We started seeing each other and sometimes he would come to mine and other times I would go round to his. He owned his own house and he was clean and tidy – you would have thought a woman lived there. He didn't smoke and he didn't drink. He also had a car – what more could a person want! You don't find many men like that around, especially not single ones.

The last photo taken of Jeremy 3 weeks before he passed away

Me with Nana Grainger
during the war

Brother John and me,
aged 4 and 6 respectively

New Beginnings

In the summer of 1979, Geoffrey asked me to marry him. I wasn't sure about this because of the age difference, so I said I would think about it. Later on I agreed, but only on the understanding that it was for the company and nothing else as I didn't want a sexual relationship. The idea of anything to do with sex still troubled me but he was quite agreeable to this, so the wedding was arranged for 3 December of that year and I became Mrs White. That was my second marriage.

We were OK for a while but he wound me up all the time. He would always be dusting behind me and he covered up the television and most of the furniture when it wasn't being used. The most annoying thing that got to me was if he was waiting anywhere with the car he always got out a duster and started cleaning his car.

One evening when I was at work Edward came into the shop to tell me that he had seen David in the pub and he had invited us all, including Geoffrey, to go for a drink. Jeff always picked me up from work and I told him about it, but he said he didn't want to as he wasn't a drinker. He dropped Edward and me off on the way home and said I would see him after closing time. I was so happy to see David, for I had never stopped loving him. We had lots to catch up on and before we left we arranged to meet up again. Geoffrey didn't mind this and later, early in 1982, he let David move in with us because David wanted to move back to Colchester as he was living in Wickford at the time and had nowhere else to live.

One Sunday things came to a head and snapped. I had put the Sunday roast on to cook while David, Edward and I went for a quick drink; Geoffrey didn't want to come. When we got back I checked on the oven and found that it had been turned off. I had a knife in my hand at the time and was waving it about at Geoffrey, when I accidentally caught him on the arm. Edward phoned the doctor, who came out and decided that I would have to go back into Myland Court for my own safety and a rest.

I was OK while I was in there, until Geoffrey came to see me. I saw him approach the house from the hall window. As he drew up he got out of the car and started to clean it, which wound me up. It was a stupid thing to do, but I was so mad that I threw a brick at his car, then I climbed in, locked the doors and sabotaged it. The staff at Myland Court coaxed me out after I had calmed down and took me back to the unit, where they gave me a needle which put me out until the next morning. Geoffrey was told not to visit me again as it affected my behaviour.

I returned home a few weeks later, but I knew things had come to a head as we were incompatible. Not long after, in 1982, I received a letter from Geoffrey's solicitor telling me that he had filed for a divorce, which was to be held on 3 January 1983 as we had to wait until we had been married three years before it could go through. It also informed me that I would have to move out of the house.

I went to the housing department to put my name on the waiting list, but we still hadn't found anywhere to go by March. Edward, who was the only one working, decided to secure a mortgage to buy a house and Edward, David and I moved into 32 Brook Street, Colchester the week before Easter.

The house was small with just two bedrooms. David and I had the largest room and Edward the smaller one. We were all happy living together and David was happy as Susan, his eldest child who had been taken into care, was given permission to visit him. His ex still wasn't letting him see his other daughter, June, and when June found out that Susan was able to see their dad, she played her mother up until in the end she relented.

Later that year David was going to decorate the big bedroom and as he was stripping the wallpaper off the ceiling the whole lot collapsed. David and I were lucky that it hadn't fallen while we were in bed, as it appeared that it was only being held up by the paper.

A couple of weeks before Christmas I received a letter from the housing department offering me a one-bedroom ground-floor flat in Queen Mary Avenue, Berechurch. I moved in on New Year's Eve 1983 at 2 Dunwich Court. I would now be able to start a new year and a new life. David moved in with me permanently three months later – I was now happy and could focus on the future.

David and I, like most couples, had our ups and downs, but I think I began to get a bit possessive as I was afraid I would lose him. We were happy together and David was more settled once we had moved in as a couple as this meant that he could now have Susan and June over to sleep at weekends. We had two pouffes that folded down into single beds which we put into the front room so they were together. They loved coming to ours, but June used to get upset when it was time for David to take Susan to catch her bus back to the children's home as it meant she had to go home as well.

After we had been together at Dunwich Court for three years, we decided to get married. I was so happy as my dream had come true at last. My friend Anita made me a lovely cream wedding dress and I borrowed her sister's veil. David's family helped with the reception, which we held at home. My daughter, who was now married to Ashley, was my maid of honour and my niece and Anita's daughter, with my 15-month-old granddaughter, were bridesmaids. It was a nice sunny day and the happiest day of my life after all the bad things which had happened in my past. The wedding went on into the early hours of the morning and everyone had a good time.

My sister, Sandra, was getting married in the November of the same year. I was invited but I declined the invitation as my mother was going and we still weren't on speaking terms. Mother now had her sister Joanne from Scotland living with her, who was always causing trouble with various members of the family. Some of us even called her the 'wicked witch of the west' and it suited her well.

Just before my sister's wedding my mother and her sister were stirring up trouble for me again. I had had enough and so I decided to put pen to paper and write to them telling them both about the abuse I'd sustained from my father. She of course said I was a liar, but Sandra said it might very well be true as he had tried to do the same to her. As she was that bit older at the time when he tried it on, she had told him that if he ever tried it again she would tell and he never went near her again. Like me, until now my sister had never told anyone until I had sent the letter and opened the doorway, so to speak.

When I discovered it had also happened to my sister, I was upset because I thought I had managed to protect her from our father.

However, as it turned out, it happened once I had left home, so it was out of my control anyway. I felt increased hatred towards my dad in the knowledge of what I had just learned. My sister and I stayed in contact right up until Mother died.

Now it was out in the open about what my father had done, I felt a sense of relief. I still felt awful about it and although I hated Mother so much, I felt better about not having to keep such a terrible secret. She wouldn't have believed me anyway, had I spoken up earlier. Nothing changed between Mother and me, despite things being out in the open and despite it having happened to my sister also. If anything, it just made it worse and I came to despise her, also. Everything was swept under the carpet and nothing was ever mentioned about it again. She would never say sorry or admit she was wrong, but I guess she didn't want to talk about it because of an overwhelming sense of guilt that she felt. I can only ever wonder how Mother felt about his memory when he died.

Edward had now moved to a larger house nearer to us and he asked David if he would do some decorating for him, which was when things began to go wrong. I didn't mind David doing this, but Edward was taking him out drinking every night when he got home from work. He was going straight to the pub from work and coming home at closing time.

One evening he came home a bit earlier from work to get ready for another night out at the pub with Edward. My temper got the better of me and I did something that I later regretted. I went round to the pub and told Edward that Neville was not his father. He was upset, even though he'd had nothing to do with Neville. He asked who his real father was and I told him that it could be his grandfather. David was angry when I told him a few years ago but this news came as a blow to Edward. David was the type of person who kept quiet about things and so he didn't say much about it, deciding it was my business and not his. Therefore he did not interfere, saying I shouldn't have told him, but he was supportive nonetheless. Of course it stirred up a hornet's nest and he rang my mother. I had already said in the letter that one of the children belonged to my father but not who it was, but she still went off on one nonetheless.

The next day my mother and the wicked witch of the west were at my door. I could see them through the window at the main door to the building, but they couldn't get in as it was operated by a buzzer between certain hours of the day, so I just ignored them until they went away.

The next day Edward went to see a solicitor to take me to court, so when I received a letter about this I replied giving all the details of what had happened. I told him that if he wished to pursue the matter I would come to see him after I came back from Berlin, where I was due to fly out the next week to help my daughter, who had just been transferred to where her husband was now stationed with his regiment. Although we'd had arguments we had been on speaking terms for the last two years, when she went to Berlin, when Rose was 2 years old. Rose had been left with me while her mother had been socialising with other soldiers. While I disagreed with what she was doing, there was nothing I could do about it. She used to go away for the weekends, leaving me an emergency contact number. She was certainly one for men, for whatever reason, and the first I learned of her adultery was when she said she was pregnant. At the time she said it was her husband's, but it turned out not to be.

I received a reply from the solicitor saying that he had informed Edward to drop the matter as I had been through enough already and I never heard any more about it. Edward and I didn't speak to each other for quite a long while after that.

Mary's Troubles

Mary came out of the care home when she was 17 years old in 1980 and she returned home to live with me, but only for a few months. Mary and I didn't get on, so she asked social services for permission to live with her boyfriend's parents, until they were married. Mary had to seek permission as she was still under social services' care until her eighteenth birthday. Needless to say, I wasn't happy with this arrangement. Before we fell out with each other Mary had been as nice as anything. At least she was until I had paid for her wedding dress, shoes, veil and tiara, then it was a different story.

A year after Mary's eighteenth birthday, Harry and she were married in the summer of 1981. I was in hospital at the time, after stabbing Geoffrey in the arm by accident. Harry's parents invited me to the wedding and they said I could stay with them until after the wedding. The hospital agreed to let me go to my daughter's wedding as long as a relative could take me. Edward was happy enough to do so, as long I went back after the wedding had taken place. Because the wedding was in Staffordshire, it meant staying over from the Friday evening to the Monday morning.

In the end, I wished that I had never gone. Mary completely ignored me the whole time I was there. I felt so embarrassed when Mary presented Harry's parents with gifts at the wedding reception. Some of the guests who were from Colchester and knew me, and whilst in my heart I knew I had bought the wedding dress, I felt uncomfortable not bringing anything with me. I wouldn't have minded if everyone hadn't turned to look towards in my direction. I was already depressed and it didn't take much to break down crying.

Edward escorted me from the room to get me a drink, but because of the medication I was on I couldn't drink any alcohol, so had to make do with orange juice. Harry followed me out to the bar and apologised for Mary's behaviour. He also thanked me for coming to the wedding and for ensuring that Mary had a nice dress for their big day. Harry took us back to the house before going back to the wedding reception. Edward and I would have returned to Colchester that night, but there were no trains until the next morning.

Later, Harry was transferred back to Colchester to join his regiment in the army. Mary followed shortly after when Harry had arranged suitable accommodation for them both on the army estate. Mary fell pregnant while Harry was away on tour in Canada. Mary had been seeing other soldiers while he was away and they were divorced soon after. Mary then married Ashley, one of many soldiers that she had been seeing, at which point she moved to a council flat on the Greenstead Estate in Colchester, where I had lived before Jeremy had died.

After I was told that Mary was going out with Ashley I was angry because Mary was married to Harry, who was serving his country in Canada with his regiment. What I didn't know was that Mary was pregnant at the time and when I found out, I naturally thought it was Ashley's baby. At the time I was told it was Harry's child and that Mary became pregnant when Harry was home on his last leave, when they were staying with Harry's family in Staffordshire. I fell out with Mary when Harry and she separated and she moved in with Ashley. Mary always wanted to make up and be friends when she wanted something and I lost count of the times she had one of her tantrums.

Mary told Harry that he didn't have to pay maintenance for Rose, his daughter. It was only later when she couldn't manage on the wages Ashley was earning in the army that she changed her mind and decided to get in touch with Harry to ask him to start paying the maintenance for Rose.

Harry agreed on the proviso that Mary got a paternity test which he would pay for. Rose was now 5 years old and she cried when Ashley took her to the doctor to have the test done after Mary had refused to take her. Ashley was sure he couldn't be the father because Mary must have already been pregnant when he met had her. The test proved that Harry was not Rose's father. It turned out to be another soldier she had been out with, and later Ashley adopted Rose as his own.

When Rose was first born Mary had contacted me to go to see her as she wanted Rose to have a nana. Rose stayed with me quite a lot and we were very close. A couple of years later Mary and Ashley had a daughter, Sharon. Ashley had already been posted to Berlin and Mary and the two girls joined his regiment after Sharon's birth. Sharon was only a couple of weeks old when they arrived there and two weeks later I joined them in Berlin for a month to help Mary settle in and to help with the children. I loved Berlin and being with the children. Rose was my life as I had practically looked after her for the first two years of her life before the family moved to Berlin. But as with her wedding, I wish I had never gone as Mary and I didn't get on and it was upsetting for Rose to see us arguing. I did have some good times when I was there, though, and I made friends with some of the army wives. We used to go round to each other's houses to play games until it was time to fly home to Colchester. Ashley and his mate took me to the airport and he apologised for the way Mary had behaved throughout my stay. Mary didn't say so much as a sorry or a goodbye.

Ashley was then stationed in Scotland, not far from Edinburgh, and Mary and the children followed. Mary and I got on if we were miles apart from each other, so we kept in touch by writing letters this time.

In 1989, Edward and I mended our bridges and put the past behind us. It was the same year I turned fifty and Edward surprised me by booking a holiday to Florida for my birthday in the October of that year. He also bought me a lovely watch, which I still have. David, my husband, didn't want to come with us. He had never been on a plane before and didn't fancy the idea of flying. It was a fantastic holiday and we went to Disneyland and to see the dolphins and killer whale. At the time it was the holiday of a lifetime; my dream holiday I didn't achieve until a few years later.

Just prior to the holiday Mary had written to me to let me know that she was having another baby, which was due in the November, asking if I would be able to go Scotland when the baby was born to help out, also inviting us for Christmas. Against my better judgement, it was arranged that I would join them on 7 November, two days after my holiday in Florida. When I arrived home David had some wonderful news to give me – Mary had given birth to a boy, Bobby, on 4 November 1989.

Missing and On the Run

My life continued as normal for a while and I was happy the way things were going between David and me for the next few years. I now had three grandchildren: Bobby, who was three days old when I first met him, Rose, who would be 4 years old on 25 January 1990, and Sharon, who would be 2 years old on 11 April of that year. Rose and Sharon were both born in Colchester hospital, both of whom were just two days old when I first saw them.

As David and I had both been invited for Christmas, I went up to Scotland as planned two days after I got home and David followed two days before Christmas. Sharon took to David straight away and was always Grandad's little girl.

The Christmas festivities went well and Edward phoned to see if all of us were having a good time. Mary and Ashley asked if Edward would join them in Scotland to celebrate the New Year, so Edward booked a seat on a plane and flew up to see us all. David and I were supposed to be travelling back to Colchester a couple of days after Christmas so we could be at home for the New Year, but Edward convinced us to change the coach tickets so all the family could be together.

What a time we had! Never again! While we had all had a nice Christmas, we shouldn't have stayed for the New Year. I went down with the flu and Mary had one of her tantrums and was screaming and shouting at Ashley because he had invited some of his army mates to spend the evening with them. It was awful and David and Edward would have gone to the pub to get out of the way, but it was New Year's Day and so it was closed, as was usual in Scotland. In the end Ashley took Mary up to the bedroom to talk to her, but it was no good as Mary started to throw Ashley's clothes out of the window. All he could do was leave her in the bedroom to cool down.

Nothing else was said about the afternoon's events that evening. Ashley's sister, Margaret, came over for the evening but Margaret got a headache and went up to bed with Sharon. I was already in bed because I had gone down with bronchitis and was feeling really ill. I was glad to catch the coach home.

My friend Maureen and I often had days out together, travelling on the bus every Wednesday to a different town to go shopping. We became 'ladies who lunch' and when the weather began to get warmer, we would go to the seaside at Walton to look round the shops and the market, before sitting near the sea and doing some knitting or crocheting. Maureen and I are like sisters. We are both overweight but it didn't bother us until later in life, when we both suffered with arthritic joints in our bodies.

On a Monday morning Maureen would come to see me at the flat where David and I lived. David made himself scarce in the garden or in the shed if it was raining as he didn't want to listen to a couple of old ladies discussing things that we had been doing when we went out together. The other days of the week I would catch up with the housework and the washing. I also did some baking, usually cakes or pies, which David and I ate for dinner.

We were always getting into trouble of some sort or other when we were out, but it was these things that helped me recover and get over the traumas from my past. Another time after we had been for lunch Angie sent me ahead to open the car doors. I pressed the key and climbed into the car. Angie had some new CDs in the car and I was quite content to look through them while I was waiting for them. I was sat in the car wondering why they were taking so long, when I heard Angie say to Maureen, 'She must be here somewhere.' I turned round and called out to them, then Angie asked what I was doing in someone else's car. I had got into the wrong car and had gone through all their CDs.

I quickly climbed out of the car and slammed the door, when I remembered that I had left my walking stick in the car. We sat waiting for the owner to come back. It was a lady who owned the car and I explained to her what had happened. I said I was sorry and she opened the door for me to get my stick. The lady was very nice about it and said that the door must have been left open by mistake. We all had a good laugh about it on the way home. We always enjoyed ourselves when we were out together.

On another occasion Angie had booked a night out to the theatre with some of the girls. Angie couldn't drink as she was driving, but she had bought some for the others to drink on the way. I don't drink, but the girls asked me to try some. I liked it and had a couple more. We met up with some more of our friends and we all went to the bar to get a drink before we went in. Cherelle, my granddaughter, asked what I wanted and I said I would just have a Coke, but what I didn't know was that she had put a double vodka in it. By the time we got to our seats I was getting a bit giggly.

The girls put me on the end so I could see better and also so I could stretch out my bad legs. The show was really funny and I was laughing so much that my false teeth flew out. I shouted to Angie that I had lost my teeth, which started everyone off – even the two women who were performing on stage. I couldn't get down on the floor to find them so Lindsey, one of the girls who was sitting next to me crying with laughter, crawled around on the floor in the dark looking for my teeth. She eventually found them and I put them in my handbag so I wouldn't lose them again as we were only just coming to the interval.

During the interval we all went to the bar and when I got there some members of the audience asked if I had found my teeth. I said that I had and told them they were safely put away in my bag. It was a good night and we finished off the evening at the pub before going home.

David was unable to go to work as he had a frozen shoulder caused by a trapped nerve. He had limited movement in his arm and shoulder and was in a lot of pain. The doctor signed David off work and it was three years before his shoulder had healed. He used to travel to the hospital every week for treatment. They tried acupuncture, exercise and injections. Eventually, the consultant suggested a cortisone injection, which was inserted into the bone in the shoulder, and within a week David's arm and shoulder were back to normal.

I remember one Easter when I dressed up as a fairy to sing and give out Easter eggs at the party we were holding. No one who knew about it apart from Elsie who was on the board of directors of The Colchester and Essex Co-op Society. The directors were going to be at the party and also a young girl who was there to entertain the members on the organ. I wasn't bothered as I was always game for a laugh.

One of the pensioners called Beatie, short for Beatrice, was 91 years old. I took to her the first time we met. She was a lovely lady who liked rolled-up fags and she also liked a drop of brandy before she went to bed. Beatie worried if I wasn't around and it was always me she asked for if she wanted anything. I was a long while getting ready that night and because another member, Patricia, whom I had known from my schooldays, had followed me out, Beatie thought I was ill. But when I came in as fairy singing she found it hysterical. Just after Beatie's ninety-third birthday she passed away and all who knew her were very sad.

This was the party piece which I would sing, changing whatever the occasion it was for – birthdays, Christmas, anniversaries, etc:

> I am your Easter fairy,
> my name is Fairy-Emily,
> And I have come to say,
> A very happy Easter to all of you today.
> I know that I am rather large,
> To sit upon your laps,
> But think of all those cuddly bits:
> A large round bottom and two large tits.
> And now, before I have to go,
> There's something just amiss,
> Ah! yes, I know what it is –
> To fly around the Co-op hall
> And give these eggs to you.

Just imagine what an 18-stone fairy would look like! Still, if it gives people a laugh that's the main thing. Laughter is the best medicine anyone can have. I joined the club when I became 60 years of age and I still enjoy my Tuesday afternoons very much.

The following summer Mary asked if we could have the two girls to stay as Ashley was being discharged from the army on medical grounds and they were going to move back to Colchester when the army had sorted out the discharge papers and the medical reports. Apparently, Mary had been advised by the doctor that Rose needed to have contact with me if she was going to get better. Mary moved in with a friend on the Barn Hall Estate to start with, but later she was given temporary accommodation in Spurgeon Street. Rose was a lot happier and joined a group of majorettes and when they had days out for competitions it was me who always went with her.

We looked after the girls for six weeks while Ashley and Mary packed up and stored their things until they could find suitable accommodation. Ashley followed later but Mary came to Colchester with Bobby so they could find somewhere to live. At the time David and I were living at the old address at the flat, so we only had room for Rose and Sharon to stay.

Rose and Sharon were no trouble and Sharon followed David wherever he went, even sitting outside the toilet waiting for him to come out. Rose was Nana's little girl as I had looked after her for the first two years after she was born in 1985. By now it was September 1989 and we had a lovely summer that year. I was able to take the girls to the park in Colchester, which was only ten minutes' ride on the bus. Colchester Park has a Roman castle, which is now a museum displaying Roman artefacts and their history with Queen Boudica. If it was wet we went to Walton Pier and David came with us. The girls enjoyed all the rides and put pennies in the slot machines. When the weather was dry, we went on to the beach first if the tide was out and then to the pier to finish the day off. At the end of the day we returned home to Colchester with two tired children.

Mary managed to find a house to rent on the Monkwick Estate not far from us and Rose and Sharon moved in with their mother as soon as she was settled. Rose was 5 years old that December and started school in the January. Mary wanted to send Rose to St George's Primary School, which wasn't in the catchment area where Rose was living, so she asked if David and I would let Rose live with us during the week. David and I discussed it and as Rose was happy living with us, we agreed to help out.

Mary had enrolled Rose to start after Christmas but in actual fact she was able to start the following day in the mornings in their nursery class.

Because there was no uniform required in the nursery class, this gave Mary plenty of time to save up to buy one for when Rose moved into the infant class after Christmas. I knitted all of Rose's cardigans for school. I also knitted some jumpers and cardigans for Sharon and Bobby. I particularly liked knitting the patterns with television characters on the front. I was always knitting something and over the years I have made many shawls, baby clothes, jumpers and blankets for friends and neighbours, as well as family. Some of them were sent to people abroad, to Egypt, Spain and America. Even now I still crochet shawls and blankets for the church, which are sold to help the people in Egypt.

I got to know the headmistress quite well as on Monday mornings the parents were invited to go to the children's assembly. I also used to join some of the mothers on Wednesday afternoons, when we planned things we could do to help fund-raise for the school. I used to knit toys and lots of different things for the school bazaar. The headmistress was so pleased that she asked if I could knit a couple of coats for her poodle and when the children left the school, my next-door neighbour's son used to bring me a letter whenever the dog needed new ones.

Owing to my increased disability, I was given a walker, which came in handy as it meant I was able to take Rose to the majorette competitions. Mary couldn't be bothered to take her so I offered; otherwise, Rose would have had to go on the coach by herself. Rose would have been six in the January of 1991 and had joined the majorettes not long after she had moved back with her mother when they were given temporary accommodation by the council housing department.

While Maureen and I were still able to walk short distances with our walkers, Angie took us both out for the day when the children were at school. One day we went to Sudbury which I will never forget, because as Maureen got out of the car, she got her boobs caught in the car and as I said, we all had a wicked sense of humour. I called to Angie to come and open the car door but she was curled up with laughter, which started me off. Eventually she managed to get the door open. I don't know how she managed to shut her boobs in the door but I do know that she had a couple of bruised boobs the next day. Maureen knows what we're like and after the initial shock, she had a laugh about it herself.

Everything was going well until Edward got into some trouble and went missing. We didn't know what he had done until his boss came to fetch the keys to the shop and the warehouse. We didn't know where the keys were but he had left a note saying he had posted them to him. Apparently, he had stolen quite a lot of money from his boss and had disappeared somewhere.

Edward had sent a letter to his godmother telling her he would no longer be in this world when she received the letter. This worried her a lot and so knowing about Edward's medical history, she got in touch with the police to report it. As Edward had been diagnosed as schizophrenic, the police came out to see me, but I had no idea where he could have gone. The police already had Edward on the police files from when he had been arrested in Scotland for the theft of a purse, although they were unable to find him. I worried about him endlessly, hoping he hadn't done anything stupid.

When Edward finally came back a month later, he was arrested for fraud. While he had been in Spain he falsely claimed that he had lost some traveller's cheques and so was sent some more. He also owed money elsewhere. Edward was given a fine and put on probation. The probation officer helped Edward find a cleaning job and a place to live. He was advised by the probation officer to declare himself bankrupt and to start living a new life. Edward went to court and he got away with all the charges.

Edward settled down and was getting on well in his job, later being given a transfer to Stevenage, where he met Linda. Linda worked for the same company in the offices. Edward used to go round supermarkets and offices after closing time to clean the floors. He was later promoted to floor manager, giving orders to the workers as well as taking the wages out on Friday to give to the staff. Perhaps now he would begin to settle down and I could get my life back on track.

Edward moved houses as he had got behind with his payments on the mortgage and subsequently rented a house with his lodger on the Broadlands Estate and got another job. We thought he was settling down, until one Monday morning when his lodger came to see us to ask if we knew where he was. The lodger, also called Edward, had received a letter from the estate agents saying they were behind with the rent, despite him giving him the money to pay it. Edward hadn't been seen since before the weekend.

I was worried, so I telephoned his workplace to see if he had turned up for work. When I got through I explained who I was and heard the person on the other end tell someone what I had said. Then I heard someone say that Edward hadn't got a mother. I was so angry that I shouted down the phone that I was still alive. They said they were sorry but that Edward hadn't turned up for work. He wasn't in any trouble, though.

This was the second time he had lied about his family, as he had told his last employer that he needed time off as his sister had been killed in a car crash. We didn't find out about this until one day when Mary's husband went to do some work for Edward's former boss. Ashley mentioned that Edward used to work for them and he said that they had felt sorry for him as he had lost his sister, Mary. Ashley was so shocked that he replied that this wasn't correct as he was married to her and she was at home.

We wondered what he could be up to now. But while he was on the run again and causing trouble, he was still my son and I was worried about him.

It was a couple of months before I found out where Edward was. During the early hours of one particular morning, the door bell went. I answered it through the intercom system and was greeted by the police. I let them into the main building and they asked me if I knew an Edward White, as he had changed his surname when I married his stepfather, Geoffrey. I replied that I did and was told that he was staying with monks in a monastery in the far reaches of Scotland. Apparently, he was due to appear in court that morning on charges of theft. They gave me the address and asked if I was able to go to court, which was a silly thing to ask as they knew that there was no way to get there in time for the court case.

The next day I let his sister Mary know and said I would advise her of any developments when I had more news. I received a letter from Edward two days later saying that he had received a fine and that he had to pay back the money he had stolen. He said that the monks had given him some money so he could come back to Colchester and that he planned to stay with Mary.

Over the next few months we helped him pay back his fine and the money that he had stolen and things seemed to be getting better. But once again we had got it wrong. He was quite lucky getting jobs, for whatever reason, it was just holding them down that was the problem, having done something stupid. When he used to get paid, he used to give me the money and I sent a cheque to pay off his fine. I also helped out with some of my own money, to help him pay it back quicker and get his life back on track. Every weekend I used to cook for him as he was living in a bedsit at the time.

The third time Edward went missing was after he had stolen a credit card and pin number that Ashley was waiting for in the post. When it didn't arrive, Ashley phoned the bank to see where it was. It was then that Ashley discovered that someone had taken £400 from the account over the last two days. Ashley wondered if Edward had taken it as he was the only other person in the house (apart from Mary) and he was nowhere to be found. Ashley came to the flat where I was living to see if David or I had seen him, but neither of us had. I later learnt that he had used the money for his gambling habit.

Later in the week we received a letter from Southend Hospital advising us that Edward was being sent to the Lakes as he was an alcoholic and needed some help with his addiction. The Lakes was a wing at the general hospital, where people were sent when they were suffering with problems like gambling and drinking, as well as the mentally ill. It was the same sort of place where I had been sent after Jeremy's accident; only the place I was taken had been pulled down and the Lakes had been built in its place.

Apparently, Edward came home at the weekend but was to leave for the Lakes on the Monday. I have no idea where Edward stayed that weekend, but he phoned to ask if I would meet him on the Monday and accompany him to the Lakes.

I met him the next day at the corner of Osborne Street as I wanted to get a weekly bus pass so that I would be able to visit him each day. He said he wanted to get a paper and that I was to wait for him. As he was going near the ticket office I gave him some money and asked him to get the pass for me, as walking was still difficult for me.

I had waited for ages in the pouring rain, when I realised he wasn't coming back. I was so angry. I didn't have a lot of money at the time as we were on benefits and I only got paid every fortnight. He had also taken the bus pass which hadn't run out and so I would now have to pay out for a new photo and a pass. I suppose I should have learnt my lesson by now. When were things going to go right for me? To top things off, I was now at loggerheads with my daughter because I had agreed to stand by him when he had got into trouble and David was also angry at the way he treated me.

Edward eventually went into the Lakes to get help for his drinking. I also found out that the money he was taking was for gambling, which had become an addiction. I went to visit him and as usual said I would stand by him.

Edward moved in with Linda and her 10-year-old daughter, Danielle, and I hoped he would settle down and keep out of trouble.

Then one day Edward came round to ask if I would like to stay the week with him and Linda so I could meet her, as Michelle was going on holiday with her father, Linda's ex-husband. David was fine for me to go and he said it would be a nice break for me. Linda was lovely and we both got on really well together. I was able to help round the house while Edward and Linda were out at work and I prepared the evening meal every night.

It was quiet and peaceful where they lived, with no noise apart from the traffic. Linda confided in me that she was worried about Edward's gambling on the horses and greyhounds. I was sorry to hear this as it was gambling that had been the cause of his earlier problems. While I had missed David, I was sad to leave the peace and tranquillity to return to Colchester. I never liked being away too long without David but he was the sort of person who liked to be in his own bed at night, which is why I go on holiday by myself; apart from the time when I went with the church group. If I waited for David to go with me I would never have had a holiday.

Edward was happy living with his partner and her young daughter, but he was very jealous of her ex-husband, who used to go round to the house to fetch his daughter, Danielle. Her ex was able to let himself in as he still had a key and was paying half the mortgage so that his daughter had a roof over her head, which didn't help matters. Linda wouldn't have been able to keep up the repayments on the money she earned otherwise, so it was a case of needs must. Linda and her ex were quite happy with this arrangement, but Edward asked her to take out another mortgage to pay off her ex on the proviso that he would help towards paying it off. But Edward wasn't able to take out a mortgage or to have any credit as he had gone bankrupt a few years back under the advice of his solicitor, so Linda took one out and everything they bought after that was in her name.

It wasn't long after this that I received a visit from the police asking if I had seen him, which I hadn't. I was told that he had gone off with the works' van. I phoned Linda to find out what was going on as they both worked for the same firm and was told that not only had he gone off with the van, but he had also tried to run her ex over. Apparently, he had phoned the shop that her ex owned and was on his way over with a shotgun to shoot him. The police had to be informed and her ex had to shut the shop and send the staff home. They had armed police waiting but he didn't turn up. He was later picked up and arrested, and he received a prison sentence.

In the meantime, his godmother who I had adopted as my mother had received a letter from Edward asking her if she would contact me to see if I would visit him in prison. I told her that there was no way I would visit and that I was so ashamed of him for leaving Linda in all sorts of debt. I disliked the way he had treated her and I disowned him like his sister Mary had, which was long overdue.

After Edward had landed himself in trouble again he was given a custodial sentence. To this day, I have no idea where he is. Edward would sometimes use the surname White, other times Turner, but it made no difference to the police – they had Edward's fingerprints on file.

I stood by Edward for his first three offences and the fact that I did so didn't go down too well with Mary, who told me that I couldn't see Rose any more as she knew that was the only thing that could hurt me as we were very close. Mary even went into the school to tell the head-mistress to deny me access to the school. But Mary was told she was making a big mistake as it would be Rose who would be hurt the most. I was old enough to get over it, but she would suffer greatly. Mary was also told that I wouldn't be stopped from going to the school as I helped them out at lot. It was hard for me, especially if I passed them on the street, as Rose would want to talk and Mary would pull her away. I was hurt and Rose would get so upset. At the end of term the family moved back to Scotland, which made it easier for me, but not for Rose.

But this wasn't to be, as I received a letter from Mary, who had written on the back of the envelope: please open this letter as it is from Rose. Rose had been bullied at school and Mary was having trouble with Rose's health because she wasn't having any contact with me. The letter was from Rose saying that her mum had given her permission to be able to write to me, asking if I would write back. It was hard as we hadn't been in contact for some time. I wrote to her as often as I could, but it just brought back bad memories. It was also making me depressed and upset.

Eventually I went to see my doctor, who arranged for me to see a counsellor each week at the surgery as she knew about my history. I went every Thursday afternoon and it felt a lot better to be able to talk about the past and get everything out into the open. Things seemed to get better after that for a while.

Despite all the problems in other areas of our lives, over this period, David and I were getting on really well. He didn't like what Edward was doing, but he didn't like to interfere. He kept himself to himself but supported me when I needed it and listened when I needed to offload. We had little tiffs now and again, but nothing more than most couples. I was frightened he might leave me with everything that was going on, but he was supportive to the end, for which I love him.

Challenging Times Ahead

In 1991, I was introduced to a lady who was to become a great friend. It was David who asked me to go and meet her. At the time he was sorting out her garden and he noticed that like me, she enjoyed knitting. He mentioned this to Maureen and she said she would like to meet me. I went to see her one afternoon and we had a lot in common, including being a bit on the large side. We got on well together and I would go to see her each Wednesday afternoon. Maureen, in turn, would come to me on a Monday or a Tuesday morning.

When the summer months came we used to go out for the day on a Wednesday to different towns, where we would have lunch and a good laugh. One of our favourite places was Braintree, where we would go to the Lemon Tree for lunch and later call in at the supermarket to buy a large cream cake. We would then sit on the wall outside and eat it.

At the time Maureen's daughter, Angela, was expecting her first child, so Maureen was busy knitting baby clothes. Because I was able to crochet, I told her that I would make Angela some blankets for the baby. Maureen asked me if I would teach her to crochet and she is now able to make circular shawls and blankets. On Sunday afternoons in the summer we met up in the Castle Park to listen to the band, taking our crochet with us.

That same year, on a Monday at about 9.00 a.m., there was a knock at the front door. I went to answer it and standing at the door was Mary. I told her I had nothing to say to her and not to come back. I wasn't going down the same path again. I wanted nothing to do with her after she had hurt Rose so badly the last time and then I shut the door on her.

David was at the shop at the time and when he got back I asked if he had passed Rose on the way, which he hadn't. He didn't say a lot at the time, but later that week he must have had contact with Mary, because they made arrangements for me to meet her and Rose.

I was angry with him for arranging it when I knew nothing about it and told him there was no way I would meet them. I was sure she would use Rose against me at some point and I was right. I'm not sure if David went to meet them to tell her that I wasn't coming as I can't remember. But after the following weekend Mary contacted David again to say that Rose had been in hospital following a panic attack. She asked if I would see Rose and said that I need have nothing to do with her if I didn't want to.

Reluctant at first, I agreed to in the end for Rose's sake. We arranged to meet up one evening and David came with me. It was heartbreaking, as when Rose saw me she ran to me with tears in her eyes. I was so overwhelmed that I was in tears as well. We decided to go for a drink at the pub, where the children could play in the garden.

I wasn't in good health myself and I was now using a wheelchair to get about. I had got arthritis in my spine and both knees and was unable to walk far. I was diagnosed disabled and was given a disability and a personal care allowance to help me get around a bit more. I was never without friends and was very much a stay-at-home person anyway, so I didn't feel like I was losing out as such.

In the summer of 1996, while I was still able to get out and about, David and I said we would take the children to the swimming pool. Rose had gone out somewhere, so we only took Sharon and Bobby. Things were going fine, until David asked if I would go with Bobby into the little pool while he played with Sharon for a while.

I was sitting on the pool steps watching Bobby, when he started to lie with his face under the water. It reminded me of the tragedy when Jeremy had his accident; he also used to do this at the pool. I asked Bobby not to do this and I was surprised and shocked by the foul language that came out and things he called me. I pulled him to one side and tried to explain to him what had happened to Jeremy, but he continued to call me all the names under the sun. I was so angry that I dragged him out of the pool and marched him over to see David, who got him dressed and took him home. I told him to tell Mary that he was not to bring him round to mine ever again as I certainly wasn't having a 7-year-old speaking to me like that.

After the incident at the pool with Bobby, Mary banned me from seeing the two girls also, so we both went our own ways and we haven't spoken to each other since. David was still allowed to visit the children, but after a while he gave that up as a bad job as Mary used to send the children out to play whenever he was there. It became clear that all she wanted was to find out what was going on in our lives. Mary was also very close to my mother, who would now talk to David, when not so long ago she didn't want to know him. I think it was more to get at me than anything else.

In the early part of November I went into hospital to have an artificial knee joint put in so that I could walk a little easier. I couldn't walk properly and was in a lot of pain. Both knees should have been done, really, but hindsight is always a good thing. The doctors were allowed to send you to any hospital as they were responsible for their own budgets, so I was sent to a hospital in Kent specialising in arthritis, rather than wait for another three years for it to be done at Colchester. I was in and out before Christmas, in time to spend a nice, quiet Christmas with David's daughter June and her partner; they now had two children of their own, Marti and Letitia. I remember frightening the life out of Marti, poor little soul, when he drove a toy truck right into my knee and I screamed in pain. I was still in a wheelchair for a short while following the operation, as the stitches had split open, which meant I had to have a nurse come in every day to dress it.

The following year I decided to visit my old school friend Olive in America, who I hadn't seen for forty-five years. I had lost touch with her when she got married, although we had seen each other twice since, whenever she came back to England. We had kept in touch by writing to each other all this time, until I had a phone installed and was able to phone her. I booked my flight for early October and Maureen and Angie took me to the airport and remained with me until my flight took off. I hadn't been abroad since Berlin and my new knee had enabled me to make this trip. I was well taken care of at the airport and was met at the other end, where I had to change flights with a wheelchair in tow. I felt sorry for the poor man who had to push me to the other side of the airport, as he was only a little guy and he looked tired and done in. I was so grateful that I gave him a large tip for his trouble.

It wasn't hard to spot Olive as she hadn't changed at all in looks. We had a six-hour car journey ahead of us, as they live in Missouri in a little place called Kirksville. I got on well with all the family and we went out a lot to different places. I remember one lunchtime when we went to meet one of their daughters and they decided to take me for a Chinese meal. At the end of the meal we were given a Chinese cookie. I hadn't had one before and so ate it all up. Olive asked me what had happened to the piece of paper that was inside. I asked her what she was talking about and they couldn't stop laughing because I must have eaten it.

I had a great time shopping in all the big stores and bought lots of presents to take home. In the big Walmart store I learnt to drive my first mobile scooter. It was so funny as I kept running into things at first and after we managed to stop laughing I finally got the hang of it. It was sad when we had to say goodbye as we had spent many hours talking about the good times we'd had when we were children. Olive promised that she would see me again, as she and her sister were planning to travel to England to see her brother, Brian, and her cousins. They came to England two years later, although I didn't get to see her on this occasion, and they hope to come again in the near future. Angie and Maureen met me at the airport with Zak, my adoptive daughter Angie's son, and he was to happy to see me, telling me how much he had missed me. Zak and I have a very special bond between us.

A Wish Comes True

One August – I cannot remember which year it was – my wish was granted when my brother, Johnny, came to see me. His son, Kevin, had phoned Johnny from Ireland to tell him that Mother was dead! Kevin was in the army at the time and his wife had phoned to tell him that his grandmother had passed away. She was also told that she was not to tell Johnny or myself, as Mother didn't want us at her funeral. As it was, I didn't intend to go anyway, but I was unaware as to Johnny's plans as we hadn't discussed it.

When he found out, Johnny came round to tell me the following morning. I think he still had feelings for Mother, where I was completely the opposite. I hated her and always would for all the mental abuse she put me through and for allowing my father to do what he did. I will never forget what she did. Johnny found out when and where the funeral was to be held and we discussed what we should do. I wanted to go, to make sure she was really dead, and I think Johnny would have liked to have gone to the funeral, too, but he didn't say so at the time. Mother was going to be cremated at Weeley Crematorium, so Johnny suggested that we should park at the crematorium in a cul-de-sac near to the entrance, from where we would see the hearse and the mourners pass, which seemed like a good idea.

I asked Angela to make a card for me and to organise some flowers. The funeral was on a Thursday and the day before I bought the cheapest flowers possible at the supermarket, which had been reduced to £2 and would keep until the next morning. I had thought about giving her dandelions, but dismissed the idea as I didn't want to upset my brother.

At about 11.00 a.m., we saw the hearse and the mourners approaching the roundabout to turn into the gates. I don't know why, but I felt quite excited. Maybe it was because I was going to wave goodbye to Mother and know that she was gone forever. I felt complete relief for the first time in years, now both my parents had gone.

Johnny and I waited for the service to start before we placed the flowers in the space allocated for Mother's tributes from the mourners. As we were doing so, I turned towards the crematorium and saw someone coming towards us. It was Uncle Henry and he asked why we were sitting near the entrance and not in the crematorium. I replied that Mother had left strict instructions that Johnny and I were not to be told of her death and that she didn't want us at the funeral.

Uncle Henry refused to take no for an answer and insisted we should join him. The bearers were still taking flowers over to the place allocated for mother. Uncle Henry passed the flowers that Johnny and I had bought to one of the bearers. I had put both of our names on the card – I could see no reason to waste money on someone who had hated me from birth – and I had written a message saying that I hoped her soul would be better in heaven than it was on earth.

As we entered the crematorium, the service had just begun and the vicar paused for us to sit. When my sister saw me her eyes dropped and she avoided my gaze. It was only when the coffin passed through to be cremated that I knew for sure that Mother was gone forever. Johnny and I did not stop to look at the flowers. Neither of our names was mentioned in the service; only my sister's, the grandchildren and a few select friends. It was if Johnny and I had never existed.

Johnny and I went out to lunch to celebrate with my adoptive mum, who had been in touch with me when she'd heard of Mother's death to see if I was all right. We picked her up after we had been to the crematorium. I heard on the grapevine that I was criticised for the wording I had put on the card with the flowers, but all I had written was that I hoped her soul would be better in heaven than it was on earth. I could have said a lot more under the circumstances …

Uncle Henry and Auntie Pat

Uncle Henry was the youngest child of my nana and grandad Chaplin. He was named Henry because he was the last surviving child of the sixteen Nana had given birth to, thinking at the time of King Henry VIII. Johnny, my brother, and I never called him uncle. He was only six years older than me and we looked on him as our older brother. Nana Chaplin worked as well and so was unable to look after us, so it was always left to Henry if Mother had to go to work or out somewhere.

As you already know, we lived with Nanny Grainger throughout the war years. Henry's favourite game at Nana Chaplin's house was to play ghosts, especially if Johnny and I were going to sleep over for the night. Johnny and I slept in the small bedroom at the back of the house. It was Henry's responsibility to ensure we got to bed on time and sometimes he would let as both stay up longer, always making sure we were both tucked up in bed before the adults came home. I didn't mind playing ghosts when were downstairs with the lights on, but at night-time, after Johnny and I were in bed with the lights off and the door closed, it was a different matter.

A short while after Henry had left the bedroom the door would open with a creak and then he would come in with a white sheet over his head. He used to have a torch underneath the sheet to make shadows with and he made ghost noises, which would make Johnny and me scream in fright. Mother and Nana Chaplin wondered why we often had nightmares ...

When I was older Henry would take me to the skating rink near the seafront. I liked skating and one year I asked my parents if I could have some skates of my own for my next birthday. Henry and I were very close and when I look back, it reminds me of Korky, David's cat – the one who used to follow David everywhere. I did the same thing with Henry and I idolised him. When I wasn't playing with my friends, Olive and Barbara, we used to go swimming together.

Later, Henry left home and went to live with his employer in Gorleston-on-Sea, on the Norfolk coast, where Henry started work in a public house as a chef. Henry was a good cook and most jobs he applied for involved cooking. Henry was always on the move, never staying in the same place for long. He soon moved to Great Yarmouth, where he met Pat, whom he later married. My uncle Arthur, one of his brothers, lived not far from him in the town centre with his wife, Rita. Rita was unable to have children and so she collected dog ornaments and called them her babies. Arthur and Rita later moved from England and emigrated to Canada. I sometimes stayed with Pat and Henry in Yarmouth, where he had settled for longer than usual. Pat didn't like dancing, so whenever I stayed with them, Henry would take me ballroom dancing at the Palais as it was the only time he got to dance.

Henry used to come to see me whenever he had been to visit my mother. I was married to Neville at the time and was going through a bad patch. Henry asked Neville if he could take me back with him to Yarmouth, to see Pat and the new baby who was now a month old, named Henry after his dad. I was off work at the time so Neville didn't object to me going away for the week. I agreed to travel down there with Henry, but what I didn't know was that he came on a moped. No way was I going to ride pillion on the back of it; I was too frightened of falling off.

Henry finally convinced me I would be safe enough, so I agreed to give it a go. We found a small case to strap to the moped and I packed light. We said our goodbyes and then I was told to hold on tight around Henry's waist and to lean right and left whenever he did. I put on the spare helmet, hopped on the back and away we both went. After a while I began to enjoy the ride. It was a long journey, so we stopped a couple of times for a rest and to go to the toilet. But by the time we arrived my backside and legs were so stiff I could hardly stand. Then I remembered that I would have to do the same again going back home to Colchester ...

Nana and Grandad Chaplin

When I went to live in Clacton with my parents and brother, I was happy to be living near my nana and grandad Chaplin. I was the eldest grandchild and they doted on me. I spent more time with them than at home. My mother was the oldest child of sixteen, only eight of whom survived. Nan gave birth to a set of triplets – three girls – but they died within three weeks of each other. She had also given birth to twins, Robert and Richard – Bobby and Dickie for short. Charlie was the next eldest in line, then there was Tommy, Arthur, Joanne and, finally, Henry, plus my mother. At the time of writing this book, the only two siblings left are Joanne and Richard. There were others but they died at birth and I didn't know their names.

Of the twins born to Nana and Grandad Chaplin, Bob went on to have two children of his own and he and Beryl, his wife, moved away from Clacton to live in a town called Basildon. None of us had much to do with either Bob's or Dickie's families and they were both known as the scruffy part of the family – the terrible twins. Dickie lived in the next road, near to where my family lived at Great Clacton. The families never visited each other. In fact, none of Nan and Grandad's children were close to each other, except Henry and my mother.

Once, Henry came to visit my mother. It was a nice day and Henry asked Mother if she would like a ride out in the car. I was fifteen at the time and my sister was four; Father would have been working on Clacton Pier. It must have been on a Sunday, because I wasn't at work. When we were on our way my sister asked where we were going. Henry told her we were going to see the Basildon queen. Mother and I never said a word; we both knew exactly where we were heading – to Bob's and Beryl's.

When the car stopped outside Robert's house, my sister asked when we would see the queen. 'In a minute,' Henry answered, then he knocked at Bob's door, which was answered by one of the children.

We were invited in and shown to the front room. Oh my God! The state of the room was appalling. It was filthy. The settee was piled high with clothes, if you could call them that, for they were more like rags. We cleared a space so we could sit down, but you had to be careful where you walked or sat as there was stuff everywhere. How could Henry bring us to a place like this? We were asked if we would like a cup of tea, but seeing the state of the cracked mugs, we all declined. The kids were drinking out of jam jars, as they didn't have enough mugs to go round.

Henry told Bob we could only stay a few minutes, as he wanted to visit more of the family before returning home to Yarmouth. All of a sudden, my sister piped up, 'Where's the Basildon queen?' Mother was mortified and unable to respond, so I stepped in and told her that Henry had said if we came when the carnival was on, she could see the Basildon queen. No one batted an eyelid. Mother was glad to leave and she berated Henry when we got back to the car. It was the first and the last time we went to visit them.

My auntie Eileen, Richard's wife, always kept the house clean, albeit a little untidy, but then that is to be expected when there are children about. The children were always clean and presentable. I don't know why Mother called them scruffy; she probably thought she was better than everyone else.

Nan and Grandad lived a few houses down the road from where I was living, so I was able to walk there by myself as long as I took care to stop at the entrance which led to the stables and made sure there were no horses or traffic coming. This entrance also led to the gardens at the back of the houses to where Nan and Grandad were living. The stables were fenced off, leaving enough space to gain access to the back gardens. Grandad's back garden was quite long, at the bottom of which he kept chickens and bantams. Bantams are a lot smaller than chickens and laid smaller eggs, but they were just as tasty. I often went with Grandad to help collect them.

Grandad also liked gardening, so there was always plenty of vegetables, even when there wasn't much meat. When we were still on rations, Nan always made the meal up with dumplings and for afters, we'd have suet pudding or spotted dick with custard, if we were lucky. I spent most of my time with Nana Chaplin when I wasn't playing in the street with other children, more often than not with my best friends Olive and Barbara. I liked playing hopscotch and we used to draw the lines with chalk on the pavement. The cat's cradle was another popular game, where a piece of string or wool was folded in half, with the open end knotted. It would then be placed on each thumb and small fingers, forming a sort of rectangular shape. The other player would then try to make another shape by transferring it onto their own fingers. We used to play it for hours, both players trying to make as many shapes as possible. We played lots of games that are still played today, such as marbles, jacks, sometimes called five stones, often on your own. Others included the whip and top or rolling a hoop along the path with a stick. Television wasn't invented in my earlier years, so in the evenings families would play board games and if you were lucky, your parents would join in, too.

Christmas was the highlight of the year at Nana and Grandad's. Nana would always be busy making mince pies and sausage rolls on the run up to Christmas. Weeks beforehand, she would pickle onions and make the Christmas pudding, with threepenny bits inside. Nana let me lick the spoon and scrape the mixture from the bowl. I always went to Nan's on baking day, which was usually on a Saturday, after Olive and I had done the errands in the mornings. Sometimes, Olive would join me and we were each given a spoon to scrape out the bowl. She always left extra mixture in the bowl, so Olive and I wouldn't fight over who'd had the most. Nan would then give us both a hot crispy roll with cheese, which had been warmed in the stove on the black range. I remember Nana Grainger having a black range when I lived with her; it was still in the house when I went to stay when I worked in Birmingham. Such fond memories! Sometimes I wish I could go back to my childhood years, but without the sexual abuse and the mental cruelty my parents had subjected me to when I was a child.

When I woke up on Christmas morning, I would find a stocking at the end of the bed. This was usually one of Father's socks, filled with a few nuts and an orange. Sometimes there would be a silver sixpence in the toe of the sock, or a tin whistle, or a soft coloured ball attached to a piece of elastic. My prize possession was a rag doll sticking out of the top of the sock and I had one every year. A lady who lived at the other end of the street made them to earn herself a little pocket money. I remember one Christmas my grandad made a battleship painted in grey. It was large and my brother treasured it for years. That same year Grandad made me a desk with a lid that opened and a matching chair to go with it. This was the only big present I can remember getting at Christmas.

Nana and Grandad often took me out with them and one Saturday I was taken by bus to Colchester. Grandad didn't have a car at the time and little did I know then that I would be living there when I grew older. He also took me to see Mr Hyam once, who used to live in Dudley Road, at Clacton-on-Sea. He used to dabble in all sorts – mainly antiques and second-hand goods, and on this occasion I came away with my first doll's pram, which was so big that it would hold a small baby. I cherished this pram until Mother gave it away to Aunt Mary, Charlie's wife, for their baby, Linda, as they couldn't afford one. I often wonder how Linda is getting on as she was taken into care, because Mary left Linda in a potato field. I heard later that Linda was adopted by a policeman and his wife; I never did get my doll's pram back. Now, there is a pawn shop in town called Hyam's – I wonder if the owner is related to the Mr Hyam whom I had known as a child ...

On Christmas morning I would walk to Nan and Grandad's with my sister and brother, while Mother cooked the dinner. We were told to be back by one o'clock. When my sister was two and a half years old, she received a doll's pushchair for Christmas and wanted to take her two new dolls for a walk. The route she wanted to take was about a mile, maybe more. When we got to Nan's, Grandad was already in the Christmas spirit and Nan was busy getting the inner ready. Nan only used the front room for special occasions and Grandad was getting it ready for the evening, when all the family gathered together. It was decorated with the usual paper chains that were stuck together by Johnny and myself, and there was a fire burning in the grate. It was a typical Christmas scene. There were nuts, tangerines, apples, dates and an assortment of sweets and soft drinks for the children. The adults had something a little stronger: port, wine, whisky, Babycham – you name it, they would have it. Nan and Grandad had saved up all year to have a good Christmas. They didn't drink all year round, apart from when they went to the comrades' club on a Friday evening, when Nan would have a stout and Grandad a beer. Sometimes we would go with them. The club had a children's room, so the adults could have their drinks in peace. Grandad would pop in to see if we were all right from time to time, bringing crisps and pop to drink.

One Christmas morning Grandad gave my sister a small drop of port and she was wobbling all over the place. I couldn't take her back home in that state as my father would have gone mad, being teetotal having seen first hand what drink can do; his own father was a drunk and he and his siblings were often subjected to abuse. The rest of my family would be joining them later in the afternoon, so Grandad told me to leave my sister with him and to tell my parents that she had fallen asleep.

When we had all finished dinner, we made our way back round to Nana and Grandad's. After tea the grown-ups played card games, like canasta and rummy. I joined in with some of them and we used to play with pennies that had been saved up during the year. Everyone was enjoying themselves, when there was a knock on the front door and the sound of children shouting. Grandad told everyone to be quiet and perhaps they would go away. It all went quiet and we thought whoever it was had gone. Nan checked the back door was locked, so if anyone came to the back they wouldn't be able to get into the house, then we all carried on as before.

The radio was on and we were listening to Christmas carols, so no one heard the back window open. The windows were sash ones and could easily be opened from the outside, by sliding the windows up. All of a sudden, five children came crashing through the front room shouting, 'Happy Christmas, Nanny and Grandad.' It was my uncle Bob, Auntie Beryl and their children, the youngest of whom was about eight months old. Unfortunately, I was left looking after all the kids and as the baby was so young, I had to nurse him on my lap. I was fed up and wanted to go home. I was thirteen at the time and thought it wasn't fair being made responsible for eight children, including my brother and sister. While I was nursing the baby, he soiled my new dress which I had been given for Christmas. I went through to the front room crying and thrust the baby into his mother's arms. Bob started laughing and I hated him for it, being young and impressionable. The Christmas day that had started so well was now ruined.

We used to call them the 'scruffy family' and I wanted to go home as soon as they arrived. It wasn't the children's fault that they were like this, as it was down to the parents. They lived in squalor and I don't think Beryl ever did any housework. The kids were always filthy, with runny noses. Nan had brought up eight children of the sixteen she gave birth to and they were kept clean and tidy, even if they had to have hand-me-down clothes, so there was no reason why Beryl's kids should be the way they were; it was just laziness on Beryl's part.

One Sunday, Nan, Father and myself went to see my grandad in hospital in northern London. Sometimes my sister came with us, but this particular Sunday Sandra stayed at home. It was just after Christmas, coming up to the New Year. It was grandad's birthday on the Sunday, though I cannot remember if it was 30 or 31 December. I was always glad to see Grandad and he would give me a big kiss and a cuddle, something no one else ever did in my family. I don't think my parents knew what love was. I certainly didn't get any and neither did they ever tell me they loved me.

While we were at the hospital, Robert and the Basildon queen – Robert's wife, Beryl – arrived to see Grandad. We all stayed until visiting time was over and as we were leaving, Grandad called me back and gave me another kiss, telling me he would always love me and be with me. He then asked me to look after Nan. Grandad passed away the following Saturday; he must have known he was dying and that it would be the last time I would see him.

Robert offered to give us a lift home as there was plenty of room. Father tried to tell him that we were fine on the train, but Robert would have none of it and insisted that we go with him. Nan looked at Father, who looked at me – standing in the hospital car park was an old ambulance, which is what we were going home in. On the way home Beryl suggested to Robert that we call in at Beryl's mother's for a cup of tea, but Nan, Father and I would rather have gone straight home. Beryl's mother lived in the posh area of London, in Ilford, and there we were, turning up in a rundown ambulance with the lettering removed.

Beryl stepped out of the ambulance then knocked on the door, but there was no answer. Then Beryl started shouting through the letterbox that she knew her mother was in, followed by a stream of abusive language that even an Irishman would have blushed at. It was so embarrassing, especially what with Beryl being a former Sunday school teacher, or so she said. It was ages before we arrived home and Mother wasn't too pleased to see the ambulance pull up outside the house with Robert and the family in tow, either.

To pour hot water onto old wounds, as the saying goes, Father always found some excuse to keep me up after the rest of the family had gone to bed and I was made the object of his sexual activity that night.

My brother, Johnny, and our sister, Sandra, didn't really get on as my sister fell pregnant out of wedlock. She didn't marry the father of her firstborn, instead marrying the man who got her pregnant the second time. She asked my brother to walk her down the aisle on her wedding day, but he refused as the child was illegitimate; my sister hasn't spoken to him since.

When Grandad passed away, Nan came to stay with us for a while, of which I was glad, as I got a reprieve from Father's sexual abuse. I was able to go to bed the same time as Nan, because Nan and I were sleeping in the same room. At the time I was working in the stockroom at Woolworth's in Clacton and it was then that I started sleepwalking. I don't remember anything, but Nan told me I got out of bed one night and cleared everything off the dressing table. She didn't wake me but asked me what I was doing, to which I replied that I was trying to make room to put some balls away. Nan said she then steered me back into bed. In the morning when I found out what had happened, I explained that the balls I must have been referring to were dozens of bags of large coloured balls which I'd had to find room for at work. It was summer at the time, which was why so many had been ordered. We'd had so many delivered that we'd had to store some in the cellar of a public house not far from Woolworths.

When I was married and we had our own council house, I was able to keep my promise to Grandad that I would look after her and she would never go into a home. Nan always visited me on Wednesdays to see the children and she used to stay for dinner. She also came on Sunday and we used to go to church in the mornings and evenings before being taken home. When Jeremy was old enough he went with Nan.

As Nan got older she used to fall a lot. It was about the time when I married Geoffrey, my second husband. Nan would only ever stay with us. Henry had offered to look after her but she declined and asked him to fetch me the first time she fell. I stayed with Nan that first night until the next morning, when I took her back to stay with us. The children had all grown up and left home, so Nan came to stay with us, until she felt well enough to go home.

Nan and I were devoted to each other. It was Nan who had taught me to knit when I was 5 years old and when I was about eleven, Grandad taught me how to knit on four needles; he used to knit his own socks. It was Nan who looked after Edward when Mary was born. Edward liked to play with saucepans and pegs, and it kept him happy for hours. But when I was in the maternity unit, poor Nan fell over them. Edward never played with them again and instead, Nan bought him some plastic toy ones to play with. When Edward was born, Nan bought me a quilted pram cover. It was a lemon yellow with blue reindeers. I still have the cover now and I keep it stored with Edward's christening gown, which all three children wore at their christening, along with Edward's and Jeremy's silver egg cup and spoon that their godmother bought for them.

Nan and I often went out for the day together. I have a terrible sense of humour and am always laughing at something. One day Nan and I decided we would go to Ipswich with my sister, Sandra. Edward was just a few weeks old, so I took the carrycot on wheels, as it was light to handle. After arriving at Ipswich, we had to cross over a large iron bridge to get to the exit to the railway station. Sandra was helping me to carry the carrycot and Nan was walking in front of us. As we were coming down the steps, there was a thud and the sound of someone rolling down the steps – it was poor Nan. I tried my hardest not to laugh, but Nan knew what I was like, often laughing at other people's misfortunes. I helped Nan up and took her for a cup of tea while she recovered from her fall. After that, Nan pushed the carrycot as it gave her some support and it was fortunate that she did, as she then tripped over the kerb and was saved from falling over by the carrycot. In spite of Nan's misfortunes, we all had a lovely day.

One year when I was thinking of going on holiday, Nan had a very bad fall and had to go into hospital. At the time Mother was talking to me and we went together to see her in hospital. She was very poorly and was expected to have to stay in for at least four weeks, maybe longer. Staff at the hospital were considering sending Nan to a residential home while they found a suitable home, but I wouldn't hear of it. I was assured Nan would be well looked after if I still wanted to take a holiday, so I decided to go ahead with it. I planned to visit Mary in Gibraltar where her husband was stationed at the time. I arranged for the sister in charge to keep Nan at the hospital until I returned, at which point I would take Nan to live with Geoffrey and myself. Mother decided to come with me to Gibraltar, but Geoffrey didn't like flying and stayed at home.

When we arrived back from holiday, we went round to the hospital for afternoon visiting, but Nan was nowhere to be seen. I began to worry, thinking she had died, so Mother went to find the sister on duty, to see what had happened. I was very angry and upset when I was told Nan was in a residential home. Apparently, my mother's sister had made arrangements for Nan to be put into a home and she had also had Nan's bungalow emptied, selling what she could.

She must have planned this, knowing Mother and I would be away. She never told anyone about what she was doing and I was devastated that I could no longer keep my promise to Grandad not to send her to a home. I felt incredibly guilty and even more so when I went to visit Nan. Nan stayed in the home until she passed away with pneumonia at the age of 92. Her death was kept from me at the time, as Mother didn't want me to know. It was one of my cousins who came to tell me. It was a September, near to Jeremy's birthday. My cousin said she would let me know the date of the funeral and I thanked her for letting me know, telling her I would be unable to go as I had just come out of hospital, after having a hysterectomy. However, when I was able to go out again, I took some flowers to the chapel where the book of rest was kept. I will miss her dearly ...

Moving On

I was not in good health by this time and I had a lot of pain if I stood for too long. I had arthritis in the base of my spine but I was all right when I had my walker with me as it had a seat attached to it so I was able to sit down. Later, the arthritis gradually crept into other areas of my bones. My right knee joint was operated on in 1998 and I was given an artificial joint. I should have had the other one done but they refused to do it as I was overweight. I have always been overweight since the age of 5. I was angry because the hospital where I'd had the first operation weren't bothered about my weight and there were lots of other patients in the same condition as me at the time of my assessment before the operation and yet they agreed to do theirs, which didn't make sense.

When I left the hospital I was given a wheelchair to use for a few weeks, until I was able to walk with a walking stick by myself. After six weeks of physiotherapy I was able to get about with my walker and get on the bus to go to town or for a day out with my friend Maureen and her daughter, Angela. When I broke up with Mary for the last time, Angela became a sort of adoptive daughter.

Over the next few months my left knee started to get more painful, as did the base of my spine. I was determined that it wouldn't stop me from going out and that I would keep walking for as long as I was able. My arthritis had started to get worse again because of my age and I needed to have a bedroom of my own because I was keeping David awake as I wasn't sleeping very well owing to the amount of pain I was in. I now had it in my feet, hips and at the base of my spine, but they weren't able to operate because I was overweight. As it turned out, it wasn't arthritis but polymyalgia arthritica, which affects the larger bones in the body, like hips, neck, shoulders and elbows, so I was in constant pain and suffered from stiffness. This condition was more common in ethnic groups, but Westerners can get it. This was about the time when we put our name on the list with the council housing department to see if we would qualify for a two-bedroomed bungalow. We were told that I would have to be assessed by one of their social workers, to see if we would qualify for one.

They sent someone out to see me and the lady agreed that I needed to be moved and that my application would go before the next committee meeting. A few weeks later we received a letter to say we had been put on the waiting list until one become vacant and as they didn't have many two-bedroomed bungalows, it was likely to take a while. David and I were happy as it meant a new beginning away from my children and all their problems. Neither did we feel obliged to tell them where we had moved.

I now had a new family, as my friend Maureen's daughter, Angela, had adopted me as her second mum. Maureen was quite happy about this as she wasn't in good health, either, and she knew that if anything happened to her I would look after Angie and the family. Angie had quite a bit of trouble with her husband and they later divorced. I didn't know her first husband as she married him when she was sixteen. After Angie had left her second partner, Sean, she then rented a little cottage in Brightlingsea and while Maureen and I were able to get about with our walkers we used to visit Angie every Monday.

One Monday we were sitting at the back of a bus with my four-wheeled shopper. The bus was just going down East Hill in Colchester, when a car pulled out in front of it and the driver had to brake sharply. I fell off the seat and onto my shopper and Maureen landed on top of me. The bus driver didn't check to see if everyone was OK and neither of us was able to get up. The bus didn't stop until it got to East Gates, where it had to wait for a train to go by and a passenger helped us up.

Maureen was OK as she had landed on top of me, but I was a bit bruised and battered. Both of us have a wicked sense of humour and when we both got over the shock, we couldn't stop laughing as all the wheels on my shopper had buckled and the frame was bent. When we arrived at Angie's, she opened the door and on seeing my shopper she burst into fits of laughter.

Angie met someone else shortly after and they decided to have a relationship. Darren was a nice young man and he visited them more regularly at the cottage, sometimes staying overnight; although he had his own house in Colchester. After a while they decided to have a baby and my third grandchild was born on 18 March 1998 – a little girl who was named Kira. Later on, Angie decided to move in with Darren. They were together for about a year, when Angie found out that he was having an affair with one of her girlfriends behind her back. Angie had helped this friend move to Brightlingsea and saw to it that she was settled in. How low could a friend stoop? Needless to say, she is no longer a friend of Angie's. Angie moved out and was given temporary housing not far from town. Angie is not an aggressive person and she takes everything in her stride.

Angie and Darren got back together in 1999 after sorting things out, at which point they moved into Darren's house in Colchester, until August 2000, when Darren was again seeing somebody else. Angie moved to Simon's Lane not far from where Darren lived. Angie is a very easygoing person and they parted on good terms. Darren and Angie are still on speaking terms and Kira sees her father most weekends and goes on holiday with him and his new wife, Jo.

Angie started to see some of her old motorbike friends, which is when she met Mark in 2001 at Snetterton Motor Racing Circuit at a Superbike meeting. In 2002, Angie moved to a new-build at Poplar Close in Colchester, where she is still living. Mark and Angie started dating regularly and they were married on 1 April 2004 at Layer Marney Towers just outside Colchester. It was a lovely day and the wedding went off well until late in the evening. Mark is a very loving person and I am proud to have him as my adopted son-in-law. He is the nicest person Angie has ever been out with. I am so glad as she deserves to have a bit of happiness in her life. Angie is a person who thinks of others before herself. A couple of years later, Angie gave birth to a beautiful daughter named Meadow, now my adoptive granddaughter.

I am lucky to be able to call her my daughter and she is always there when I need her. A couple of years after they were married Angie and Mark had a beautiful daughter and they called her Meadow, so I now have three beautiful granddaughters: Cherelle, Kira and Meadow, and a precious grandson, Zak. I love them all equally, but I have a special bond with Zak. It's probably because he was so like my Jeremy when he was younger and I would like to think that Jeremy would have grown up like him. Zak is such a gentle boy and very loving and caring. I think he takes after Angie for that.

In 1999, just after my sixtieth birthday, we heard from the housing department asking us if we were interested in taking a bungalow with the Guinness Trust Housing. It was the Easter holidays, so we had to wait until after Easter until we could go to see them. We went the following Tuesday and were told they would make arrangements with the Guinness Trust to get in touch with us. The bungalow was in Pioneer Close, but we had no idea where it was. One of David's mates knew most of the new estates, so he took David to see where it was and it was right near the town centre, just off Golden Noble Hill, where the old Co-op warehouse was. They had a look through all the windows and round the back while they were there. It was semi-detached and tucked away in a corner on its own. We met the officer from the Trust and he showed us round. We said we would take it, signed the papers and moved into number 5 on 19 April – our wedding anniversary. I now had a chance to start a new and happy life with the man I loved.

Angie, My Adopted Daughter

I first met Angie when I was at Maureen's during one of our knitting sessions. Angie was in Maureen's back garden with her partner, who was fixing a bike at the time. When I saw who Angie's partner was I was flabbergasted, as he was a bad lot. I had known him since he was born and his parents lived on the same estate as us in the 1960s. His name was Sean and he was born the same year as my oldest son, so they were both at school together. Sean had two older brothers. When he was younger, he had to be pushed around in a pushchair for quite a while as he was disabled. Eventually, he was given a wooden leg and he was always referred to as Peg Leg, which he was fine with.

Angie lived with Sean for two years and they had a daughter, Cherelle, before they were married Cherelle is now my eldest adopted granddaughter. After they got married in 1982, they started having problems in their relationship and Angie had quite a time of it. Sean spent most of their benefit money on drink in the local pub, coming home at all hours of the day and night drunk. Maureen often used to lend Angie money for things for the baby and she found a house for them to rent a few doors away from where she lived. Sean even took the money that Maureen had given Angie, once again frittering it away on drink. A couple of years after Cherelle was born, Angie gave birth to a boy, Zak, who is now my adopted grandson.

Angie and Sean then moved to Longridge Park, a small estate near Greenstead Estate, because the owner of the house they were living in had sold it. This was when things started to get really bad. By this time Sean was an alcoholic. He was drinking more and more and was getting increasingly violent. Things came to a head when he threw a fork once, narrowly missing Cherelle, so Angie had no choice but to leave. Zak was terrified of his father and it was years before Zak would let any man near him. Angie found a little cottage to rent in a small seaside resort called Brightlingsea and Maureen gave her the deposit until Angie was able to get herself sorted.

One day, when she knew Sean would be out, Angie hired a van and moved into the cottage, with the help of a friend. Sean never found out where Angie and the children had moved to. It was May 1996 that Angie left Sean and she had no contact with him until she moved backed to Colchester after she had met a new boyfriend on New Year's Eve, called Darren. Cherelle was now 6 years old and Zak was four. Angie granted Sean access to see the children once a week, on a Saturday, until Cherelle came home one day and told her mum that Sean was taking them to the pub when they were in his care and he was smoking smelly fags that turned out to be cannabis. Angie sought advice from her solicitor and an arrangement was made for Sean to have supervised contact on a Saturday afternoon with someone from social services. But he abused this privilege by continually not turning up and eventually the children got fed up and didn't want to see their dad. Gradually, Sean deteriorated and passed away with liver failure in late December 2011.

At this point Angie was working in Colchester a couple of evenings a week as a bar person. Maureen and I used to stay over to look after the children as Angie was unable to get back to Brightlingsea until the first bus from Colchester the following morning, so she used to stay overnight at a friend's. Cherelle was now at school and Zak was at nursery, so Maureen and I got the children up, fed and dressed, ready to go to their respective places by the time their mum came home.

Grandchildren

Cherelle is the oldest of my adopted grandchildren and she is quite a character. At the time of writing this book, Cherelle is now twenty-two. I nicknamed her the knicker-watcher when she was younger, because when she was about two and a half years old she used to look under the doors in the public toilets, trying to find Maureen, her biological grandmother. She used to say, 'That's not my nana; she's not got black knickers on.'

One day Cherelle decided to paint Rocky, the family dog, with nail varnish, including its claws, and then blamed it on Zak. She even blamed Rocky once when she was in trouble for drawing on the walls. When she was fifteen months old, Cherelle took a mixing bowl out of the kitchen cupboard then got hold of a wooden spoon, some flour and eggs. She was so quiet, but when we went to investigate you should have seen the mess! Both Cherelle and the kitchen floor were covered in flour and eggs. 'I was only making a cake,' she said innocently. It took ages to clear up the mess, but you couldn't help smiling.

More recently, she went to get a top-up on a sunbed as she was going abroad on holiday with her partner, Byron, and she wanted a tan before she went. Twelve weeks into the course, Cherelle phoned her mum saying that she still hadn't got a tan and she queried it with the assistant. It turned out that she was standing in the cupboard behind the door to the tanning room – only Cherelle could do that.

I call Zak my little yum-yum boy, because when he was very young I used to play yum-yum round his little ears, pretending I was eating them all up. He used to think it was terribly funny. On a really cold day during the winter, Zak used to come home from school saying, 'Nanny Emily, my ears are cold. Will you yum-yum them for me?' If he saw me when he was out and about he would still want me to yum-yum his ears, even now at eighteen; though I doubt he'd like to admit it.

The most embarrassing thing that Zak did was when the family was still living in Brightlingsea. He had just turned two and he and his mum were waiting in a queue at the post office, most of whom were elderly women. His mum had just bought a friend a present for his birthday and she gave Zak the tin to hold to keep him quiet. Zak managed to pull the ring on the can and out popped a blow-up doll. Zak shouted for his mummy to look and everyone turned and looked in disgust, as they were nearly all elderly. Angie didn't know where to look and as soon as she had paid for the items she wanted, she was out of the door like a shot.

I love all my grandchildren the same, but Zak is special as he has the same temperament that my Jeremy had. I am very proud of Zak and when he took up karate he always won a gold or silver cup or a medal in competitions. Mostly, though, I am proud of him for his caring and gentle nature when he is with other people, especially with his grandad Roger. They were very close from the moment he was born. Roger was in poor health from the age of twenty-one, when he was diagnosed with heart trouble and was unable to work. Instead, Maureen, his wife, went out to work while Roger stayed at home to look after the two children, Angie and Mark. Mark was adopted by Roger and Maureen after they fostered him at a few weeks old.

I wonder how many boys of Zak's age would look after their grandads these days. Most boys would be out playing and messing around with their mates or worse. Zak used to change Grandad's sheets, make his bed and wash his hair. He even helped him undress for bed. Sadly, Roger had a couple of strokes early in the year 2012 and on 20 June his heart gave out and he passed away. The night he died he had rung Zak to ask if he would come and help him to bed as he was feeling poorly. Usually, Zak would have been there, as most nights he would sleep over to help Maureen and Roger, as Maureen was now severely disabled and could hardly get about. Zak did what he could for Maureen but it was Kira who largely helped her and Cherelle went round on her day off to wash her hair and give her a shower, so I am proud of all my grandchildren and rightly so.

The night of Roger's passing, 20 June, was very sad for everyone, but especially for Zak, as he was with his grandad when he died. Zak thought that his grandad had had another stroke, so he phoned for an ambulance straight away before going downstairs to tell his nana, who of course was unable to do anything. Zak then phoned his mum, who went straight to the hospital to wait for the arrival of the ambulance. He then went upstairs to hold his grandad's hand, who smiled at him before passing away. Zak was devastated and he took it very badly. In the end he had to go to see a counsellor, but I am glad to say he is now getting better.

There is not a lot I can say about Kira, except that I love her very much. Kira was always a stubborn child from an early age. She wasn't like the other grandchildren at all, who would lie on my lap with their little heads snuggled up against me and fall asleep straight away. Not Kira – she used to scream the place down. She takes after her dad for that. Meadow also takes after her dad, Mark. But the others take after Angie. Unless you cross her, she is gentle and patient.

Kira is now a typical teenager, who never cleans up after herself unless you nag her. She is very untidy and shares a bedroom with Meadow, often trying to blame her for the mess. I get on very well her and if I ask her to do something she never gives me any trouble. She also likes a cuddle from David. I think sometimes she feels left out of things, but she is lucky in a way as she has two birthdays and two Christmases – one with her mum and Mark, and another with Darren and his parents. Angie and Darren take it in turns each year. One of them has Kira on Christmas Day and the other on Boxing Day. Angie is easygoing with all her children and she often lets their friends have sleepovers. Kira wasn't a pretty baby and she was bald for quite some time. She had really blonde hair when it did finally come through and until it grew, she looked like a little boy, but she is now growing into a lovely young lady.

Meadow is the youngest of my grandchildren and I call her my little honey bee, because she is always on the go. I first saw her when she was a few hours old. She was a beautiful baby and is growing into a lovely child. When my adopted sister Maureen and I go to see her, Meadow always runs to me for a hug and a cuddle. She also wants to climb on my lap. She calls Maureen Nanny Knit-knit because she's always knitting. Meadow isn't able to sit on Maureen's lap, because Nanny Knit-knit has more spare tyres than lap. Maureen takes it all in good fun.

Meadow calls me Nanny Em-Em. It was my fault as when she was learning to speak I thought it would be easier to say than Maureen.

Meadow is quick to learn as she has her sisters and brother to help her, especially Kira. When Meadow was about 3 years old, I was sitting in the car with her once, when I cried out in pain. Meadow asked me what wrong and I told her that I had cramp in my feet. Her answer was that we would have to build a house for them. When Angie got in the car, Meadow said to her mum, 'Mummy, Nan-Nan's got the crabs.' She's never lived it down.

After that I had to be careful what I said because while waiting in the queue at the supermarket checkout, I said 'ow' again and Meadow shouted to her mum who was packing the shopping, 'Mum, Nanny Nan-nan's got crabs again.' The lady in the next aisle gave me such a funny look, until I explained what she was talking about. Meadow is now 6 years old and doing very well at school.

Dreams Fulfilled and Camel Mania

After the incident with Mary over Edward when Bobby had upset me at the swimming pool, Mary told me I would not be able to have any contact with Rose. I disowned the whole family and have not seen any of them since that day. Mary takes after my mother. I never referred to my mother as a mother, just as the person who had given birth to me, who never had time for me. In the end I was better off without Mary or my mother.

David and I settled down nicely in our two-bedroomed bungalow and it was a lot easier for me, apart from not being able to get in and out of the bath. The Trust removed the bath and installed a shower, solving the problem for us. By this time I couldn't do much lifting but was able to unpack the boxes and put the crockery away. I had always wanted to have a garden with a wishing well and lots of animal ornaments and plants. Here, I could now have my dream garden. Things couldn't have been more perfect.

We became friendly with the neighbours opposite, Elsie and Sidney, and we were invited to their wedding in the September of 2001. It was more myself who valued their friendship as David is a person who likes his own company. I tend to find I can make friends with almost anyone and our new neighbours were very good to me. They had a car and used to take me out shopping as David doesn't drive. I was given driving lessons when I was married to my second husband, Geoffrey, and I wish I had kept the lessons up. At least then I could have been a bit more independent and not had to rely on other people.

Christmas and New Year soon came and went and it was the year 2000 before we knew where we were. A new century had begun and I wondered what it would hold. That year we had a lovely summer and I spent most of the time sitting in the front garden, reading a book or knitting and doing my crochet.

In 2001, our neighbours went to Egypt for a holiday. I had always wanted to visit Egypt and so when they came back they said that I could go with them the next time.

In June 2002, I got my wish and went to Egypt. David didn't want to come as he didn't like the idea of flying, but at least now I might get to see the country and fulfil another dream of riding on a camel. When the three of us arrived it was so hot I thought that I was going to pass out. It was a bit frightening at first as there were lots of policemen standing about armed with guns. Sidney and Elsie climbed into a taxi to take us to the hotel and Elsie asked the driver if he would open some of the windows. I couldn't stop laughing as there literally weren't any windows in the car. We had just pulled out of the airport terminal, when all of a sudden the driver turned round to Elsie and Sidney and asked, 'How many camels for the big mama?' I couldn't believe my ears. Sidney told him I wasn't for sale and Elsie couldn't stop laughing.

Our hotel was right in the centre of Luxor. It was very nice and I had a room with a big double bed and air conditioning, which was lovely and cool. Later, after we had showered and changed, we all went up onto the roof where the swimming pool was and had something to eat and drink at the bar. Elsie had been to Egypt before, so she knew several of the Egyptian staff at the hotel as she always went back to the same hotel each year.

The following morning, after breakfast, we went to see some people at a shop that she had got to know over the years. I was introduced to all of them and then we were invited to sit down before being offered drinks. We all had cold drinks as it was so hot. I got on with all of them and one of them asked me if I would be his mum as he had lost both his parents in a car accident when he was a child, so I now had a newly adopted son called Ashraf. We text each other every week even now and sometimes he calls me on my birthday and at Christmas. He and his three brothers and sister had been brought up by his grandmother and an aunt.

I had always wanted to ride on a camel, so I was taken to the West Bank and got my long-awaited camel ride. I managed to walk quite a bit as the climate was favourable for my arthritis, thus making a camel ride possible. I asked Sidney to take some photos as I wanted to prove that I had been on one and I also wanted to send some to my sister and to Olive in the USA. Sidney was supposed to video it, so we could watch it when we got home, but he was laughing so much at me on the camel that he forgot, so we went back the next day to get another camel ride. But when they brought out the camel there was no way I could get on it as it was a lot bigger than the one I'd had the day before. I was standing there trying to tell the Egyptian that it was too big, when our taxi driver called out to him. The next thing I knew I was being carried by this Egyptian man who could only have been about 9 stone wet through. He lifted me up in the air easily and placed me on the huge camel. Sidney, Elsie and our taxi driver were bent over with laughter as I was 18 stone at the time.

I eventually got some photos taken and it was the most exciting holiday I'd ever had. We went to lots of different places and I could have been sold countless times for varying amounts of camels as the Egyptians like big women and blondes. I was almost married off to one who was only 25 years old. I was sixty-two at the time – I should be so lucky!

I was sorry to have to leave to come home as I had made so many friends. I even cried when we said goodbye, but I promised to go back the next year. When I got home I had lots to tell David and plenty of photos to show him – and of course the video, of which I still have a copy. If I am feeling down at any time I get it out and watch it, to remind me of the good times I'd had.

Foreign Horizons

When I returned from Egypt I spent the next few months at home, without much of a social life, but the following year, in 2003, I persuaded David to come to Egypt with me and our neighbours. He usually stayed at home as he didn't like going away on holiday. He was used to his home comforts and didn't like sleeping in a strange bed. The only times he had ever been abroad before was Amsterdam, France for a day and Belgium for a week.

We went in the June of the same week that England would be playing for the World Cup. When we went down to the shop, I introduced him to the boys. He couldn't believe that they were able to watch television in the shop and that he was able to smoke. The next day it was England that would be playing their match and the boys asked him to go and watch it with them. David got on well with all of them and he liked Ashraf a lot. Ashraf asked me if David knew that I had adopted him and I told him that he did and that he was fine with it.

In the mornings we would swim in the pool at the hotel. It was very hot in Egypt and worse at midday. I had told David to put plenty of suncream on as he burnt easily and he said that he had, but he can't have done as when we arrived at the shop that evening he started to act strangely. Seif, the head of the shop, said that he thought that David had sunstroke. He went and got a lime off the tree and told us to make a drink with it. We were on our way out at the time to get our evening meal at the English cafe where we always went and when we arrived, we asked Sidney and Johnny if they would make up the drink for David, which they did. David ordered a meal but didn't much feel like eating it.

Later that evening when he was in bed he became a bit delirious and was very hot. After he had slept he felt better but he had burnt his legs so badly that they were now beginning to blister and had opened up and were bleeding. He said he would be all right as we were going to the Valley of the Kings to see the tombs, so we went anyway. I knew that he was in quite a lot of pain but he still managed to walk around.

After we had been for our evening meal, we went back to see the boys at the shop. Seif asked how David was and we told him about David's legs. Ashraf took a look at them and asked if he would like to see a doctor. David said that he would, so he asked Seif if he could make an appointment. He was told to go straight away, so Seif hailed a cab and then sent Ashraf and Goffer, the errand boy, with David.

The doctors in Egypt are open until about 10.00 p.m. every day and when we arrived it was like one of those backstreet places you see on films. His surgery was up a load of stairs and David managed to get up them with a little help from Ashraf and Goffer. When they reached the top there were lots of Egyptian people waiting to see the doctor. There were no empty seats, so Ashraf told Goffer to tell one of the patients to vacate their chair and give it to David. But no sooner had he sat down than Ashraf opened the doctor's door, said something to him in Egyptian and then called David in.

Ashraf explained what was wrong and translated for David. David couldn't believe what he saw next, as the doctor offered Ashraf a cigarette and an ashtray while he examined David. David was given some cream and was told to go back on the Sunday to see him. He was also told he was not to go out in the sun.

The morning after David had been to see the doctor I told Elsie that David wouldn't be able to go on any more trips. They had already booked a trip for that day, so I said that I would still go with them. We always booked a taxi and usually had the same driver. I found out later that our neighbours had been ripping me off. Each time we went out, they told me what I owed as we used to divide the fare between the four of us. I had it on good authority about how much fares cost and how they were worked out, which was nowhere near what I had paid them.

I didn't say anything to them, only that I wouldn't be going out on any more trips. I was very angry as I had paid for their holiday as well as they said they couldn't afford to go at the time and it wouldn't have been the same without them. I had even given them £1,000 spending money as well as paying for their meals. They turned nasty after this and when they got home they never spoke to us again. I had been a good friend and helped them out lots of times when they had needed money. If I was to count it up the figure would run into thousands. David knew nothing of this as I would never have heard the last of it.

Following our disagreement, later that year in the October, they did a house exchange with another couple and moved away. That was the last time I would help anyone ever again – once more, I had learnt my lesson the hard way.

David didn't go out at all for the rest of the holiday apart from to see the doctor, as he was unable to get about and was having to use his hands and feet to move around the room. I arranged for him to have room service and the hotel staff were very good. Even the female cleaner once asked him if she could help him undress and help him into the bath. She cried every time she saw his legs and when it was time for us to go home she asked me if she could kiss him goodbye. We gave her a good tip and a photo which I had taken of them together; she was so pleased.

I guess the two-week holiday in Egypt was a disaster, really, what with David's sunstroke just two days into the holiday and the truth coming out about our neighbours. I even bought David a walking stick as he was still in a lot of pain before the time we were due to go back home. The skin was starting to split on his legs and it was no ordinary sunburn where the skin peels off. It was a very uncomfortable journey home for David. His legs were covered with dressings and he wore a pair of my support stockings to stop the dressings from slipping down. It's also another reason why David doesn't like to go abroad.

The holidays that we had in England were few and far between and you could probably count them on one hand. While David enjoyed our holidays he was always glad to get home to see his cat and to sleep in his own bed.

A new family moved in shortly after Elsie and Sidney moved out called Jean and David, with their adoptive daughter, Lisa. Jean was Lisa's great-grandmother, as Lisa's mother was unable to look after her properly. Her father, Clayton, Jean's grandson, was also incapable of bringing up Lisa. Jean and David had also raised Clayton, because his own mother, also named Jean, had married and the new husband didn't want to bring Clayton up and both children would have been put in care if it wasn't for Jean and David. Lisa was 10 years old when Jean and

David moved in and she had been spoilt by her mother. Jean's children were now grown up and married, but she loved Lisa as one of her own. David had MS and couldn't walk so used a wheelchair to get about. He was also diabetic.

David and I got on well with our new neighbours. Like my own husband, David was very quiet, where Jean would speak her mind. If anyone upset her she wasn't short of swearwords or shouting, mainly at her family. Jean sometimes asked us if we would keep an eye on David if she was going out and she would leave him dozing in his armchair. He was a quiet man who enjoyed a conversation with us.

In the summer months I would often sit with Jean and David in their front garden as the sun never shone in ours until late afternoon. One afternoon when Jean's husband was in the garden, Korky ventured over towards him and kept rubbing herself against his legs, which was unusual as normally she didn't go near anyone. I found out later that animals can tell when someone is unwell, which explains her behaviour.

Sadly, Jean's husband passed away in November 2007. Jean and I are still good friends and we always have a natter whenever we see each other in the garden. It was mostly David who saw her as I hardly go out unless I have to, especially during the winter months. Lisa is now grown up and got married on 4 May 2011, on her eighteenth birthday. It was a lovely wedding and the sun was shining brightly. The day went well until the evening, when David and I were ready to leave. On the way out, I missed my footing and tripped over the step. I fell down, hitting the side of my scooter inside the reception area. As I fell against the scooter I twisted sideways, hitting my head and back. It was a while before I could get up and I wouldn't let anyone help me. I was better doing it myself as I had a special knack of getting back up, which involved rolling over and getting up like spider on my feet and hands – rather a funning sight, I assure you.

When David and I finally made it outside, the sole of David's boot fell off as we started to walk home. He ended up walking home in his socks, all the way through the town centre. Even on my scooter I still arrived home before David. Jean said we should take them back to the shop we bought them from. What she didn't realise was that he'd had them for twenty-five years; they were the ones he had used to get married in.

David's Cats

David was very much a cat lover. We both liked cats but we always referred to them as David's as they wouldn't come to me unless they were poorly. I was once told that cats and other animals who felt poorly would always seek me out as I have what they call 'healing hands'. We were particularly fond of Korky, who was very special to David and myself, and now that she is gone we miss her very much, which is why I have included a chapter here about his cats.

Over the course of our marriage David has had five cats, the first of which was a tabby called Bubble who we had until she died having kittens before he was able to get her neutered. Her brother, Squeak, belonged to my son, Edward, who couldn't be bothered to look after him properly. He was a tom cat and he disappeared just after David and I moved from Brook Street to the flat in Queen Mary Avenue.

The third cat was a tabby named Muffin – another tom cat; David liked the tabbies best. Muffin was a docile old thing and would go to nearly everyone who came to visit. He would let anyone sit with him as long as nobody tried to move him.

The next cat David had was a black-and-white one called Twinkle. It was his daughter Susan's cat originally, but she went away one weekend, leaving the cat shut in by itself. It was the summertime and very hot. When she rang, David asked her where she had left Twinkle and was told she had been shut indoors with no windows open so she couldn't wander away. David was fuming and as he had a key to Susan's flat, he picked Twinkle up and brought her back to stay with us. Susan wasn't really interested in having a cat – it was just a novelty to her while it was just a kitten – so that is how David came to have Twinkle.

The last cat David had was tabby with four white paws and white under her chin. She was called Korky and on her back was a white arrow. Initially, we thought he was a tom cat when he first came to live with us, but in fact he was a she. Korky was a wild cat as the mother was kept outside in the garden and was never allowed in the house. The poor cat was always having kittens and they kept accumulating because its owner hadn't had any of them spayed or neutered. The RSPCA had offered to do it free, but the lady had refused; what happened afterwards no one seems to know. Korky was quite a nervous cat and it took David a long time before she would venture out from wherever she had hidden herself. David used to leave her food in the place where she was most likely to hide, behind a large unit in the main living room. Gradually, he coaxed Korky to come to him and once he had done so, Korky never left his side, following David everywhere.

The cats were probably the main reason why David didn't like going on holidays at home or abroad as he didn't like leaving them with anyone; although he had plenty of offers to look after them. Korky went into the cattery a couple of times but David was never happy about leaving her and so didn't let her go again. As Korky got older she thought she was the boss; although she never ventured out of the garden unless David was with her. Korky was spiteful with other cats and went wild if any dared to come into the front garden. The other poor cats tried creeping along the wall, their little legs going as fast as they could once the wall came to an end. Korky liked to sit on the step and watch what was going on. The bungalow where David and I were living only had one door which was at the front, and David used to leave this open unless it was raining so he could go in and out whenever he chose.

Korky was a fussy eater and would only eat Whiskas cat food and a certain brand of tinned tuna. If she was given anything else it was left until David put Whiskas down. I made a terrible mistake by giving Korky a tin of John West tuna as a treat once. The next time I bought a tin of Princes tuna, she wouldn't eat it. Anyone would have thought she could read the labels.

Korky's favourite hiding place outside was under a large curry plant in the front garden and whenever Korky came back into the house you could smell curry on her fur. Korky lived the longest of all the cats we had and she reached the ripe old age of 20, at which point David had to have her put to sleep as she was very ill and was unable to stand. Korky died the day before Michael Jackson and David buried her in the back garden under the curry plant.

My New Families in Egypt

One year I decided to buy myself a mobile scooter so that I could get around more as my arthritis was gradually getting worse and I was finding it harder to walk longer distances. Maureen also got one later on, so we were still able to go out together. We even started to go back to church, which we both enjoyed. The lady president who took the service was called Irene and did a lot of charity work over in Egypt with her husband, Ray, helping the poorer families. The church held raffles and other evens to raise money so they could pay to bring water to the villages and to buy things that the poorer families couldn't afford.

I was most interested in the work that they did and became involved by knitting baby coats and blankets for them to take over to Egypt. Irene and Ray usually went to Egypt three times a year with some of the church members, so the following year when they went in the August I asked if I could go with them as they were going to Luxor, where my adopted son, Ashraf, lived. I also wanted to see the work that they were doing. There were a few of us going and our holiday and work with the villagers fitted in well.

At first I wondered if I would be able to get about and I worried about all the walking with my increasing disability. However, I was assured that the airport staff would take care of me and that anyone who was unable to walk through the gate to the plane would be escorted on one of the buggies specially made for the passengers; there were also wheelchairs that could be used.

I texted Ashraf and told him I was going over and they were all excited. I bought lots of presents to take over for the boys and their families – mostly watches. As I didn't want to put them in my case, I decided to carry them in my hand luggage so they wouldn't get lost. On arrival, the group was always met by one of the airline managers, who knew of the work which Irene and Ray had been doing for some time. After I had collected my luggage, I went through customs but got stopped to be searched. I started to panic as I had fifteen watches in my hand luggage. I was trying to tell them they were gifts, when the airline manager came over and told them to let us through as we were with Irene and Ray's group.

After we left the terminal we were met by Irene and Ray's son, who was married to an English girl they knew. We all piled into the taxi and were taken to the hotel, where we were given our room keys. I had a room on my own next to Irene and Ray, with a balcony. It was a lovely hotel and in each of our rooms were a basket of fresh fruit and a plate of biscuits. In the corner of the room was a fridge with bottled water, Coke and 7UP. It was only our group that was given this treatment and Irene was referred to as Lady Irene by the staff. They had always used the same hotel and were well known for the work they did.

I got washed and changed then dropped off the presents at the shop. They were all happy to see me and greeted me with big hugs and kisses. I stayed for a while to catch up on the news and then went back to meet the others.

After breakfast the next morning we went back to our rooms to get ready to meet up at ten o'clock so we could go to one of the villages. It was certainly an eye-opener to see how the really poor live and it makes you think that in England we should be really grateful for what we have and not be so wasteful. The Egyptian people are very happy even though they don't have much in the way of material items. The children are so happy with what we take over for them, like clothes and books and pencils to use in school, unlike the youths of today who seem to expect and want the next and latest best thing out on the market, to be like their friends.

I remember one village we went to was like somewhere time had forgotten. In one of the houses the eldest sister was looking after her other brothers and sisters, while the youngest was a 2-year-old boy who was deaf and blind. He wore hardly any clothes and what he did have were rags. It made me cry to see them. They had no beds and were sleeping on planks of scaffolding.

We sorted out some clothes for them and left them some money for food. We told them we would be back to sort out water for them and to bring them beds and mattresses to sleep on. They now have water and it is a much warmer home they live in after some windows were put in. It is very hot in the daytime but cold to the Egyptian people at night, so I am sure they must be very grateful.

We had the evenings to ourselves and the group had a lot of fun as well as going out to help the poor in the daytime. In the evenings I used to spend my time at the shop with those I now refer to as my family. I even tried my hand at belly dancing, much to the amusement of all. There were shrieks of laughter from everyone as I have big boobs which were wobbling all over the place. But I was enjoying myself and everyone else was enjoying it, too. It is something I will never forget and when I hear of anyone grumbling, I tell them that they should go to see the poor side of Egypt if they feel they are lacking in any way.

When I first arrived the heat was so hot I thought I would pass out as I wasn't used to it. But I did get used to it and believe it or not, my arthritis gave me no pain the whole time I was there. I was able to walk just about anywhere and on long journeys I travelled by taxi. For health reasons, I would like to live in Egypt, but money and age prevented me from doing so. Then there was David. There was no way he would have agreed to live in Egypt, besides which he doesn't like the heat. But it was nice to walk in comfort without pain, though, even if it was for such a short time.

When the plane was getting towards London, the arthritis came back, probably because of England's damp climate. I always looked forward to going to Egypt and I went again in the October and the following February. Irene and Ray were only going for a week in the February, but I stayed on for another week. Everyone made me welcome and on the last evening before I came home Seif, who was in charge of the shop, told me that I was now one of them and no longer a visitor. His wife had made me another birthday gateau with fresh strawberries and cream. They even sang 'Happy Birthday' in their own language and again in English.

I went again to Luxor in the August, again with the group, and this time I shared a room with Joan, who also belongs to the church. There was also a member from another church who came with us. His name was Richard, who we all knew very well. Richard was always teasing us in good fun, especially myself and another member of the group called Gloria.

Gloria and I were both big, buxom girls and one morning the three of us got up at five o'clock to catch a ferry to the West Bank, the other side of the River Nile, as we were going to have a ride in a hot-air ballon. I was afraid of heights, but it was something I was determined to do. It was OK getting into the basket, as it was lying down on its side on the ground. I was really scared at first, but once we were up in the air it was really breathtaking and the experience was something out of this world and I would do it again any day.

While it was easy to get into the basket as it was on its side, Gloria and I had such a job to get out. I was OK as I had worn trousers, so I didn't mind when one of the Egyptians climbed into the basket and lifted my legs and the other one on the outside got hold of my arms as together they lifted me out. But poor Gloria had worn a skirt and as they did the same to her, Richard called out them to hang on as he wanted to take a photo as she was showing her knickers, but she took it all in good fun.

One evening after I had got back from one of my new families, the group was waiting for me in the lounge as they wanted me to go upstairs to the bar where the entertainment was being held after midnight until the early hours of the morning. I said that I was going to my room first and I was gone quite a while, so Joan, who I was sharing with, came to see what I was doing. I was just about to go down, but Joan said that I should go ahead of her and that she would just be a minute as she needed to do something. She said she would bring the key down with her.

Later, as we were in the upper bar, Joan said that she was going to go up to bed and that she would leave the door unlocked for me to get in later. The rest of the group stayed up a lot later and when we'd all had enough we all went to our respective rooms. I didn't put the light on so as not to disturb Joan. But as I was about to get into bed I saw someone's hands on my pillow and I started to scream blue murder.

All of a sudden I heard Ray singing the song 'You Need Hands' by Max Bygraves and the others laughing. They were all listening at the door waiting for me to get into bed. I pulled back the bedclothes, to see that Ray had made it look like someone was in my bed. I opened the door and Ray asked if he could have his hands back. We were all in fits of laughter. Joan had come up earlier so that she could get the key off me. I never saw them hiding behind some posts in the hallway when I went back downstairs. Like I said – we had plenty of fun as well as helping the poor villages.

Living My Dream

The same fortnight that I went on the balloon trip I was also invited to the shop owner's daughter's hen night and the wedding the day after. I stayed overnight after the hen party, as it was quite late when it finished and the family wanted me to stay for a meal. Joan was quite concerned because I hadn't returned to the hotel, and she went to tell Ray, but Ray told her that I would be all right as he knew I was with one of my new families. He rang me the next morning as Joan was still worried. I was just finishing my breakfast and told him I would be back shortly and that I would meet them in the dining room. I returned to taunts of 'You dirty old stop-out. Where have you been all night?'

I had a drink with the group and then we all went up to our rooms to get ready to visit some more villages. We usually got back to our hotel about 3.00 p.m. so that we could have a shower as the roads were dirty and dusty. Some of us went for a swim or to have a sleep. I decided I would have a sleep as I was going to have another late night tonight. I set my alarm to wake me at five o'clock, as I was due to meet up at the house and join the family for the wedding.

It was such an experience. Weddings in Egypt are nothing like those we have in England. The bride and groom have to parade through the hotel, escorted by bands and music, until they reach a platform where two decorated chairs are placed ready. They had all sorts of different rituals to perform and after that the bride and groom partook of their first dance in the hotel gardens. I sat with the main family but I was surrounded by little boys who wanted my attention. It is the boys who like to be around you rather than the girls. I think that's because the girls aren't allowed out during the daytime whereas the boys are. One little boy whom I had met at the house told the others that he was looking after me. He was 11 years old and was called Islam. I explained to him that he could look after me for the evening but that he would have to share me with the other boys. He took me up to the bride and groom so that I could dance with them and the groom put a tray on my head with lighted candles on it and asked me to dance with him and his wife.

Ashraf wasn't allowed to sit with me as all the women and children had to sit together. The women aren't allowed alcohol but we had plenty of cold drinks. They don't have a wedding breakfast like we do and instead we were given a snack box with two small sandwiches and a piece of gateau in it. Now I knew why we had had a meal before we went.

A couple of days later I had to do it all over again as I was invited to one of the staff's sister's hen night and wedding. By the end of the first week I was exhausted.

I spent a lot of time at the shop owner's house as his wife and I got on very well with each other and she rang the shop each day to ask me to join them for a meal with the little boy who had looked after me at the wedding. I called her Big Mama as she was big and cuddly. Islam came every day after school to the house to see me and to have a cuddle. One evening he asked me if I would like to go to his house for a meal and I said that I would if his mother had agreed. Big Mama phoned later to confirm the details for the following evening.

I met him the next evening at his aunt's and was taken to their house by taxi. I had met his mother several times and felt at home right away. Throughout the evening Islam kept whispering to his elder sister. I asked her what he wanted and was told that he wanted me to sleep overnight at their house. I told him that I couldn't as I hadn't got a nightdress with me. He sat with me for a while and then all of a sudden he vanished and came back with the said item which he had borrowed.

I phoned Ray to let him know that I was staying out all night and that I would meet them all at breakfast time, as Big Mama's husband was going to take me back to the hotel in the morning when he dropped the boys off at school. He had one son who was still at school and three daughters. Before I left that morning Islam gave me one of his school photos, which I now keep in my purse. He didn't want to go to school but I told him that I would see him later that evening.

I wasn't able to see Islam that evening as they heard that day that one of their relatives had passed away and they had gone to the funeral, but he came the next evening to see me at the shop. It was only a couple of days before we were due to go home and the night before we left he cried because he didn't want me to go. I gave him a big cuddle and explained that I would visit again in October. I was sad to leave as it had been a most enjoyable experience.

I did go again in the October and I thought that would be the last time that I went as I was unable to walk long distances, but I lost weight and managed to go three years later. I still keep in touch with Ashraf and the boys each week by text even now. Soon after I heard from Ashraf to say that he had met a girl and was getting married in the July. He wanted me to go, but I was unable to as I couldn't walk far or stand for too long because of the arthritis at the base of my spine. I was very sad about this, but as Irene and Ray were going to visit Luxor, I was able to give them some money to give to him to get what he wanted. They agreed to take it over there for him as they were once again visiting the villages. He sent me a beautiful photo of his wife; she is very beautiful and her name is Abeir.

By October 2006, I knew that I was putting on a lot of weight, as when I was going to the hairdressers my scooter had a job to climb the hill. When I came out from my hair appointment I decided to call into the mobility shop on the way home to order a bigger one. The one that I had only took up to 18 stone, so I decided to get one that took up to 25 stone. When I got in I told David that I had ordered a larger scooter. His reply was that I would now sit in that chair and put on more weight. I decided then and there that I would go to see my doctor, to see if she would refer me to Leap, which is a programme where you go to the leisure centre and exercise in the gym. David said I wouldn't do it, so I proved him wrong and decided to set myself a goal to aim for. My target was to lose weight so that I could go back to Egypt to see Ashraf and Abeir, who now had a daughter. Her name is Shahd, but they have nicknamed her Little Emily, so in effect I now have another granddaughter.

My excess weight was putting a strain on my joints and I was struggling to walk. I was having trouble with my breathing and had to use my asthma inhaler more often. The gym was hard work but I was given a programme to suit my ability and then was seen by my trainer every three months to be weighed and to see if I could increase my exercises. I also had to see my own doctor each month to see if I was losing weight. The doctor was pleased when I went as in the first month I managed to lose 4 lb. When I first went to the gym I could hardly walk down to where the gym was and I was out of breath, but by the third month I was able to walk there easily and I was walking better overall. I enjoyed going to the gym and went every day. I met new friends and it got me out of the house. The doctor was pleased with how much I was losing and my health was a lot better. I was even able to come off one of my blood-pressure tablets and I was no longer using my asthma inhaler.

In April I was able to go back to Egypt to meet my new granddaughter, who was now six months old, and to meet my daughter-in-law, Abeir. I had worked hard to achieve my goal of returning to Egypt and this was to be my last holiday there. I was met at the airport by Ashraf and Wael, one of the boys from the shop. We dropped Wael off at the shop and then went on to Ashraf's house in a little backstreet, where I was going to stay for the fortnight. The whole family was waiting for me as they all knew that I was coming. There were hugs and kisses all round and all the children wanted cuddles. All the families live near to one another and there were a lot of family members in Ashraf's family. I loved Grandma and she was so funny, especially when she smoked her home-made pipe, which was made out of a glass jar called a bong. I got on well with them all and was able to make them all understand me, even though they didn't speak any English. It was mainly the men who spoke English, apart from the womenfolk who went out to work.

Ashraf had arranged for my own personal taxi each day as his brother-in-law worked for a taxi firm. It was a posh taxi, not like the one that I rode in on my first visit to Egypt. Ashraf's sister had also just had a baby and he was one day old. Women had to go and stay at the family home after they'd had their babies and they couldn't go outside until there was a new moon. Their husbands weren't allowed to stay with them and had to go back to their own home at night. Another strange thing I learnt was that an aubergine was hung over the doorway where the mother was staying. I was told that it was to stop the mother from losing her milk if a stranger visited her.

With the help of his family, Ashraf had built his own house and was able to move out of his grandma's. It was a lovely place with all modern equipment. It had a shower and a flush toilet, not that I was bothered as I have been to lots of houses that still had a hole in the ground. One day when I was at the shop I asked Ashraf if I could have the key to the shop's toilet which was out in the back yard. I was OK until a lizard-like thing ran down the wall and across my feet. I screamed blue murder and ran out while still pulling up my knickers. When the boys came to see what the matter was, they couldn't stop laughing and when Ashraf came home he told the entire family in his own language what had happened and they were all laughing, too. It was a good job I don't get embarrassed any more.

I was now classed as an Egyptian and lived like one, eating the same as they did. I enjoyed being with the families as we had lots of laughs. One day I caught a little boy who remembered me from last time – which was four years ago – whispering to Ashraf. I asked what he wanted and Ashraf told me that he wanted me to take out my teeth like I did when I saw him last time. He had remembered and he was only three at the time. His name was Mokhta and he never left my side the whole time I was at the house. He would be waiting for me every time I came. He used to like sitting on my lap and being cuddled. He was a lovely little boy and if I could have brought him back with me, I would have. We both cried when we said goodbye, but I have lots of photos of him.

It was a wonderful experience to be given the chance to live with an Egyptian family and I felt more at home there than I did in England. I would have liked to live there all the time if I had been a lot younger as the climate suited me and was good for my arthritis. I got on well with Abeir and when it was time for me to go home she didn't want me to go. I was sorry to leave at the end of my holiday, but was pleased to see Mark, Angie and Meadow waiting for me when I got back. Meadow spotted me first and came running over to me with open arms.

After I returned from Egypt I continued to go to the gym until the end of October, when I had to give it up as the arthritis in my toes and feet had got so bad and I could hardly stand on them, let alone walk. I was disappointed as my health was a lot better and I had managed to lose 3 stone in weight. I knew that I would put it back on just sitting around the home, but I was forced to admit defeat. By this time the arthritis had spread to my hands and wrists also.

David was doing all the household chores and I tried to help out where I could, but David said I was too slow. This remark made me feel useless and very depressed. I know David didn't mean it to sound the way I took it, for he is a very caring person and looks after me very well. But I suppose it was also the pain I was in that was getting me down and not being able to do much for myself.

In the end I resigned myself to staying indoors when it rained and going out on my buggy when it was dry. When I had any appointment Angela would take me if she was able to do so. I still do my crochet and knitting to stop my fingers from getting stiff; although I am slower now because of the pain. I read a lot and I also have my computer to keep me busy.

On Fridays Angela takes me over to her home with her mother, Maureen. She also takes me to get the weekly shopping. Most supermarkets have buggies for disabled customers. Without Angela and my buggy, I would be almost housebound. David and I go to the pensioners' club on Tuesday afternoon, where I am the committee secretary. The club is five minutes away from where I live and I can still go if it rains as I have a rain cover and the buggy can fit in the meeting room there.

You Can Choose Your Friends, But Not Your Family

At Easter in 2009, I was feeling really unwell. I had felt unwell for some time, wanting to sleep all the time. I was becoming increasingly depressed each day, but I didn't want to see the doctor, because I didn't want to have to take antidepressants, knowing what they can do to a person. I had taken them years ago, when I was married to my first husband, Neville. But I took them for so long that they began to make me look haggard and my adoptive mum became worried about me. When I saw a photo of myself I decided that I would stop taking them. I did eventually manage to come off the antidepressants, apart from when I was at Myland Court, where I was taken for mental illness following a breakdown. Fortunately, I have not had to take them since, as once I married David, my life changed and I was happy for the first time in my life. Lies and gossip told by the rest of the family still got back to me, but I soon learned to ignore them when David and I moved away to the bungalow.

My brother, Johnny, called to see me over Easter and I told him about the symptoms I had. He sent me straight round to the doctor as soon as the surgery opened. The symptoms I described were the same that he'd had when he had been diagnosed with diabetes. I made an appointment to see the doctor, who took more blood tests. That evening, the doctor rang me to tell me he had made me another appointment for the following morning at 9.00 a.m. I was to have nothing to eat after 9.00 p.m. that evening until I had seen him the next day. I was allowed to drink, but apart from that I was nil by mouth. I was given more blood tests and the doctor arranged a further appointment for the Monday morning, once the results had been received. It turned out that I was diabetic. My blood sugar level was twenty eight and it shouldn't have been any higher than six or seven.

After that I was forced to change my lifestyle completely. With medication and armchair exercise, I lost 4 stone. My answer to the problem was to not have the food in the cupboard I couldn't eat; the philosophy being that if it's not there in the first place, you can't eat it. My sugar level went down quite quickly, only rising if I ate anything I shouldn't. I was still allowed my weekly treat, scampi with a few chips, and David now tells me I don't eat enough and that a bird would eat more. Being diabetic, other parts of the body are prone to other symptoms, as I discovered when having regular blood tests, when I was diagnosed with a lazy thyroid that wasn't working properly. This meant taking more medication. If I was to list the things that were wrong with me we'd be here all year; my mother-in-law would have said that if I was a horse, they would have shot me. I am now taking thirteen different lots of medication. If I take any more, I will rattle.

Now I am older, I have a job remembering things. I have trodden many paths to reach where I am. Since Mother died I have had a better life and hopefully I'll enjoy a few more years to come, God willing! I don't do much in the way of going out, except to Tuesday club, necessary appointments and church. I don't know what I'd do if I didn't have my adoptive daughter, Angela, taking me out shopping and on little outings with Maureen – Angela's biological mother and my best friend. Maureen calls me her big sister and lots of Angela's friends ask if Maureen and I are sisters as we look so alike.

Whilst I love David very much, some things you cannot talk about to a man – it just isn't the same. I really miss my adoptive mum. I could talk to her about anything from the age of 10. I wish I had told her about my parents years ago; maybe then I would have had a better life. I know I was born for a purpose, but I am still not sure what. Maybe it was to help people less fortunate than myself. I like to see people looking happy and if I can put a smile on their faces, it makes me feel good inside.

After losing weight, my gums shrank and my false teeth became loose. They kept falling out, so I made an appointment to see the dentist three weeks before Christmas 2011, so I would have them in time for the Christmas break. On the Wednesday before Christmas, I made my way to the dentists to collect them. There were two people in front of me waiting for appointments and I was early, so I sat down next to a young girl who had a small child with her. While we were waiting, two people entered the waiting room – an elderly gentleman with a rather large woman I took to be his wife. There were only three seating spaces in the waiting room, which were all taken. The old gentleman looked frail and was leaning on his walking stick. He looked to be in a lot of pain. Being polite, thinking the gentleman needed the seat more than I did, I stood up to offer him mine.

'Emily, sit down,' he said.

I sat down, wondering how he knew my name. As far as I was aware, I didn't recognise him. I assumed he must be someone who knew me from my past or a passenger from when I worked on the buses in the sixties. People often said hello when they saw me. How does the saying go? 'Once seen, never forgotten'.

The large woman looked at me in anger and said, 'Don't you know who he is?'

'No. Should I?' I answered.

She turned and shouted, 'It's Ashley. I am your daughter, Mary.' Pointing to the child and his mother, she added, 'And that's your granddaughter, Sharon, and my grandson.'

I was flabbergasted. Mary had put on so much weight and Ashley had aged several years. He looked older than I was. I can honestly say I really didn't recognise any of them; I hadn't seen them for fifteen years. I had seen Sharon a couple of times, but only after David had pointed her out and she had completely ignored me. She always spoke to David, though. I just used to ignore it. It didn't bother me either way, as I had disowned them all when we stopped speaking to one another years ago.

I'd heard that Sharon was married to a soldier, but that they were now separated. The child was between the age of 2 and 3 years, called Alfie. I still get to hear things via the old jungle drums, not that I'm interested.

On my birthday in 2012, Angie and some friends decided to take me to a pub, where they were putting on a performance of drag artists. I had never been to one of these shows so didn't know what it was about and what to expect. After a meal, Angie put me in the front row so I could see them better. There were three of them, one of whom was called Crystal Gale. The one I took a fancy to was named Jessica James, who was supposed to be straight-faced and serious at all times. He was short and a little tubby and when I saw him I couldn't stop laughing, especially when he came on dressed as a Telly Tubby. I laughed so much my teeth flew out and hit Jessica on the foot. The rest of evening he really took the juice out of me, making me laugh all the more.

As it was my birthday he got me up beside him to sing 'Happy Birthday'. He asked me my age and when I told him I was seventy-three he told me I was looking so good that I could still earn a living standing on the street corner under a lamp. At the end of the evening Mark, the publican, asked if they would come again and Jessica said that they would as long as I would be there, so the next time they went the girls and I made sure we were there, too. The first thing that Jessica did when he arrived was to pop his head out from behind the stage curtain and shout for me. I do miss those evenings as Mark has now left the pub.

When my brother moved back to Colchester, I was near enough to be able to visit him on my scooter and it was then that I went back to my roots and learnt the truth about my background. I visited him in his new flat shortly after he moved in and while I was there, I spoke to John about the time Angie had given me a reading in his presence. In the reading, she had described Grandfather Grainger as having he had a turban on his head and John confirmed that this was true. He had once seen scars on my father's back and Mother told him that Nana Grainger gave him the cat-o'-nine-tails (a whip they used in those days) for thieving cigarettes from the little shop where we used to get ice cream when we lived with her during the war. My nana used to own the shop until she sold it to a friend. Following the theft, this particular friend left it to Nana to deal with Father rather than involve the police.

Apparently, Grandfather Grainger was a Sikh from India, who had moved to England to live in Birmingham. Nan and Grandfather lived in a rough area, where incest in the community was rife, so I guess my father didn't know any better. My father loved me in his own way, but as it was the wrong way, as Western cultures forbid it. I hope that one day I will be able to forgive him and that time will heal. My faith has taught me that you should forgive everyone who has wronged you.

But I will find it harder to forgive my mother for the part she played in all this, as she hated me since birth and was never going to let me forget how much hatred she held towards me. She knew what my father was doing and that it was wrong and yet she never attempted to stop him or to intervene. Nonetheless, I will try to forgive her because of my faith.

We are now in 2012 and I am sorry to say that I have now put the weight back on. I now have to use my inhaler again as I get out of breath just walking a few steps. I know that I am not perfect, but who is? Each day the pain is getting harder to tolerate and different problems keep coming up, but I wouldn't change things for the world.

These days I spend most of my time indoors if the weather is wet and windy. I like Sunday because I enjoy going to church after I was stopped teaching the younger children because I had divorced my husband. I went to the Christian Spiritualist Church, where I was given a lot of help when Jeremy passed over to the other side to be with the Heavenly Father. The president who ran the church, Bernard Balls, and a medium, Maureen Flynn, were the first two people who came to see me when I was taken into Myland Court when I tried to commit suicide. I was made very welcome there and everyone was friendly. I continued to go to the Spiritualist Church and had many readings which have since come true. Lots of people think that we sit in a circle holding hands, listening out for spirits, but this is untrue. It is an ordinary church, where we sing hymns, say prayers to heal the sick and to watch over the countries that are at war. We are all God's children, whether we have two feet or four, and we said prayers for the animals, too.

One of the mediums, Peter, told me I could write a book and become a committee member. I told Peter I didn't think so but it came true years later. It was after I had been to see a counsellor, who told me the best way to help me put the past behind me was to write it down as it would be a form of therapy. I never intended to write a book but thought, why not! It would be something else I might achieve for myself. If it got published, it would also let people like Mary and her children know what I had been through during my lifetime. I have arranged in my will for someone to ensure a copy of the book is passed to them when I pass into the Heavenly Kingdom.

I had quite any unhappy childhood but on my life's journey I have met lots of people and have made some good friends. I think that it was God's will that I trod this path, as I now have the most wonderful family whom I love and treasure, and they love and respect me in return. I also have a wonderful adoptive mother who has always been there when I needed her. I am sorry to say that 'Mum' is now in a nursing home, but

Angie takes me to see her when she can. 'Mum' is a very private person and is very independent. She doesn't like people around her but I love her very much.

The most important person in my life is of course my husband, David, who is my full-time carer. He works very hard looking after my every need as well as doing all the household chores. He never complains and the only time he goes out is on a Friday night for a few hours with Allan, one of our neighbours whom I worked on the buses with in the 1960s. Since David and I have moved away from my original family we have had a happy life. The saying goes that 'you can choose your friends but not your family', but I was able to disprove this theory and prove that you can choose your family.